# Praise for Beyond Reason

"Incredibly powerful and moving."

—**Dave Isay,** MacArthur and Guggenheim Fellow, Peabody Award winner and author of *Listening Is an Act of Love*

"A beautiful story, beautifully told."

—**Joseph Chilton Pearce,** author of *Crack in the Cosmic Egg, Magical Child,* and *The Death of Religion and the Rebirth of Spirit*

"*Beyond Reason* dramatically portrays a physician's transformation, through the death of his son, from the typical 'reasonable' mind-set into the experience of mystery and magic. The story is powerful and the insights, profound."

—**John W. Travis, MD, MPH,** and author of *Wellness* and *Wellness Workbook*

"A powerful, moving story—sensitively told. From a gifted child's tragic death emerge unexpected blessings, revealing how he had as much to teach in death as in life. A story that challenges some of our fundamental assumptions about the nature of reality."

—**Peter Russell,** author of *The Global Brain* and *From Science to God*

# Beyond Reason

*Lessons from the Loss of a Gifted Child*

## GREGG KORBON, MD

iUniverse, Inc.
New York   Bloomington

Beyond Reason
Lessons from the Loss of a Gifted Child

Copyright © 2009 Gregg Korbon

iUniverse books may be ordered through booksellers or by contacting:

iUniverse
1663 Liberty Drive
Bloomington, IN 47403
www.iuniverse.com
1-800-Authors (1-800-288-4677)

ISBN: 978-1-4401-2397-9 (pbk)
ISBN: 978-1-4401-2399-3 (cloth)
ISBN: 978-1-4401-2398-6 (ebk)

Library of Congress Control Number: 2009910393

Printed in the United States of America

iUniverse rev. date: 7/15/2009

To Kathryn, who sustains us

# Contents

# Preface

I WROTE THIS BOOK for two reasons. The first was to help me understand the miraculous chain of events that happened when my nine-year-old son, Brian, died. In honor of his memory, I have made the account as accurate as I could (changing some people's names to protect their privacy). Part I tells Brian's story and, when I finished it, I thought I was done. But the mysteries kept happening, and I kept trying to understand, so I kept writing. Part II tells the story of what happened afterward: how I found gifted teachers and had so many more amazing experiences that I could no longer believe anything was impossible. As a result, the magic I thought I had lost in my childhood returned to me—one of the many gifts that flowed from the emptiness that Brian left in my heart.

Sometimes people enter our lives and change us forever. When, through their deaths, they bring us closer to God, we call them martyrs. For me, Brian was such a person. Before he died, I was a clever person adrift in a seemingly meaningless and tragic world. But Brian changed all that, and I think it might be helpful for others to know about him and what he taught me. This was my other reason for writing this book. So, for anyone who wants to know how grieving the death of a beautiful and gifted child can become a journey of wonder and hope, I offer our story.

# Acknowledgments

ABOVE ALL, I THANK my wife, Kathryn, for putting up with this book project and with me. To tell our story in an understandable way, I had to reveal many of our most personal experiences—recalling some of our most painful and gut-wrenching moments. So my appreciation, again, for all her support and patience in helping to get this story told.

When you write about something as personal as the death of your child, especially when there are so many unusual occurrences, people are usually at a loss for words. Because of this, it was difficult for me to get honest criticism of my writing. Luckily, I found three people—all talented writers and creative forces in their fields—who saw my weaknesses and gave me the opportunity to improve. They are Peter Russell, Joe Pearce, and John Travis—and I am grateful for their help.

# Part I

Beloved child, who ran
joyfully into the night,
Neither death, nor darkness
shall diminish your light

—Inscription on Brian's headstone

# Chapter 1
# Brian's Story

IT WAS A BEAUTIFUL spring day in the Blue Ridge Mountains of central Virginia when nine-year-old Brian Korbon dashed across home plate, scoring the first run of his Little League career. He ran to the dugout beaming with joy, flashed his father a thumbs-up, and gave high fives to his coach and teammates, and then—he collapsed. The next day, the wire services carried the story across the country: "Boy Dies Playing Little League." The local newspapers reported some of the details surrounding his death. One headline read, "Final Day of Young Life Spent in Triumph over Fears." The Rev. Jesse Jackson read the article and called the parents to comfort and pray with them. Paul Harvey also called and then gave some of the account on his radio program. Most of the story, however, was never told. That boy was my son, and I would like to share his story—a story that has brought comfort and wonder to all of us who knew and loved Brian.

## BRIAN'S CRAZY BIRTHDAY

Brian was our first child, and the pregnancy had been perfectly normal. So my wife, Kathryn, and I were totally unprepared for the nightmare that was to come. We were both in our early thirties and had been married for two years. Both of us were excited about the arrival of our first child, and I, having grown up as an only child, wanted a big family with lots of kids to play with. I was an anesthesiologist at the university hospital, but we decided to deliver our baby at the community hospital because we thought it would be quieter and more comfortable.

We had chosen a female obstetrician who was well recommended, and Kathryn wanted an epidural to relieve the pain. Epidurals are my specialty. I wrote books and gave lectures about them, but since I did not have medical privileges at this hospital, one of the anesthesiologists on the staff would do the epidural when the time came. Compulsive to a fault, I had planned everything as well as I could. But my plans would not be enough to protect us from what was to come.

Our problems began when Kathryn went into labor in early January. When we arrived at the hospital, we discovered that our obstetrician was out of town. We had not met the doctor who was covering for her, but he seemed pleasant enough when he came to our hospital room. Only as the day wore on did we realize that something was wrong. The obstetrician, Dr. X I will call him, promised Kathryn the epidural but kept coming up with excuses, so she never got it. Kathryn was in great pain for many hours, asking for the epidural. Every time I spoke with Dr. X, he said that he would order it, but he never did. It took me most of the day to realize that Dr. X was lying to me. He was behaving strangely in other ways as well, saying one thing at one visit and something completely different the next time we saw him. Only later did we learn that Dr. X was insane with schizophrenia; he would lose his medical practice in the following weeks. While his mental illness was common knowledge to the doctors and nurses on the obstetrics floor, no one mentioned anything about it to us.

Despite this craziness, the labor itself seemed to be going well, and then, finally, it was Kathryn's time to push. *Thank God*, I thought, *at least now I can relax a little.* But this was not to be either. Kathryn pushed Brian out, and Dr. X held him up for us to see. Then he gave baby Brian to one of the nurses who put him in a bassinette, and then they all turned away to help Kathryn. So I was the only one who noticed when a few seconds later, Brian stopped breathing. My secret fear during the pregnancy was that I would have to resuscitate my own child, and that was what happened.

With alarm, I called for help and placed the oxygen mask over my baby's tiny face and ventilated his lungs, fighting back my shock and fear. *This isn't supposed to happen*, I thought. *Fathers shouldn't have to do this.* But I had no choice. After a few minutes of resuscitation, Brian's heart rate returned to normal, and he began breathing again. But he never turned pink like he was supposed to; he remained blue. I felt a sick, sinking feeling in my stomach as I realized that something else was terribly wrong.

Kathryn and I wept when they took Brian away for transport to the university hospital's neonatal intensive care unit. The next morning, the cardiologist put a balloon-tipped catheter into his heart and tore a hole between the upper chambers, giving him enough oxygen to continue living. She told us Brian had "transposition of the great arteries," a condition caused when the two arteries carrying blood out of the heart are connected backward. Brian could live like this for a few months until he grew big enough to have corrective open-heart surgery. Meanwhile, we had to wait and deal with the constant fear that we might lose him.

Three days later, still numb from the trauma, we took our little blue baby home. His oxygen level was barely enough to sustain him (a normal blood oxygen pressure is 95, while Brian's was 24), and he was a pitiful sight. The hair had been shaved from half of his head so the doctors could find more veins to stick. He had bruises all over his body from the needle punctures, and his right leg was black because of blood vessel damage from the heart catheterization. Still, we felt grateful to have him. If he had been born twenty years earlier, we learned, Brian would have had a slow and awful death.

Although he was a beautiful baby, over the next few weeks, we kept discovering other things wrong with Brian. He had slight defects of his left ear and thumb. Later, we would learn that he was deaf in his left ear and hard of hearing in his right. Much more troubling, however, the breathing passages in his nose had not developed properly. (A baby can only breath through its nose.) Brian would struggle for every breath, especially while he was sleeping. The ear, nose, and throat specialist we consulted could not risk the corrective operations until after Brian's heart surgery. How ironic that to be a good anesthesiologist, I make sure my patients are breathing normally before I leave them in the recovery room. Yet, every night at home, I watched my own tiny blue infant fighting for every breath, and I was powerless to help him.

Our pediatricians told us to keep Brian from crying as much as possible because that would lower his oxygen level even further. But Brian developed colic, screaming in pain for hours every day and turning purple. And then the ear infections started, one every week or two—causing fever, pain, and more crying. Kathryn, who had always needed nine hours of sleep, was getting only two or three and spending days every week in doctors' offices with a screaming, scary-blue baby.

At five months, Brian became lethargic because he was no longer getting enough oxygen to his brain. It was time for his heart surgery. So Kathryn, Brian, and I flew to Boston Children's Hospital where we entered into a whirlwind of activity as we admitted Brian to the hospital, met the medical team, and checked into a nearby hotel. Early the next morning, we took Brian to the operating room and handed him over to the anesthesiologist for his surgery. A nurse took us to the waiting room where we spent four anxious hours waiting for news. (We knew the operation carried a 5 percent mortality rate.) Meanwhile, in the operating room, the surgeons cooled Brian's body down to sixty degrees and reconstructed his heart (thirty-two minutes of suspended animation with no blood flow at all).

Finally, the surgeon, Dr. Castaneda, appeared and told us that everything had gone perfectly. Then, an hour later, we saw Brian in the intensive care unit, and he was *pink*. We rejoiced. Kathryn and I had been so frightened, and now, for the first time, we allowed ourselves to celebrate our son's future. He would live! The surgeon told us that Brian might get tired more easily than other children, but, otherwise, he should have a normal life.

Other parents in the hospital told us that it takes two years after surgery to get over your fear, and it was true. This was a busy time as our daughter, Lyn, was born, and after a few weeks, she also developed bad colic—screaming almost every waking moment for nine months. Then, when she was one and still not able to roll over by herself, we learned that she had cerebral palsy. Kathryn and I were devastated. It all seemed so unfair. Why were such terrible things happening to our children? I felt empty and completely out of luck.

Lyn needed lots of special attention: trips to the rehabilitation center, physical therapy, speech therapy, and more. Meanwhile, Brian needed other operations, ten in all before he was five. More difficult than all the surgeries were the countless needle sticks, hours spent in waiting rooms, and bad-tasting medicines. Brian was a brave little boy through it all and did his best to cooperate, even when the procedures hurt him.

During this time, we were concerned with his development. He was slow to walk and talk and seemed clumsy. Had Brian's brain been damaged by his five months of low oxygen or the thirty-two minutes without any blood flow during heart surgery? We were always looking for clues. What else was wrong? we wondered.

## OUR LITTLE BOY GROWS

One encouraging sign throughout all our troubles was the brightness in Brian's eyes. They would twinkle and dance—filling us with delight. His bright, hazel eyes and broad smile would catch your eye. They could captivate a room full of people and often did. Brian's handsome face had delicate features and was framed by light brown hair. He was of average height and so skinny that you could count all of his ribs.

One early hint that Brian had special gifts was his excellent memory. When he was two and a half, he recognized a picture of a distant cousin he had met once when he was only twelve months old. "That's Mike," he said, surprising us all. He memorized his storybooks and could recite them word for word, doing all the voices with great expression—making me laugh as he did.

Brian was always entertaining us with jokes and stories and was quite a "ham." He had a splendid imagination and could make up tall tales that would fool just about anyone. Brian's poor first-grade teacher never knew which of his stories to believe. One time, his best friend's mother called to ask if it was true that I had just been arrested for having overdue library books. Another time, when Brian was five, Kathryn took him to the country store. He stayed outside to talk with a group of teenage boys while she shopped. When Kathryn returned a few minutes later, Brian had the teenagers spellbound. One of them approached her very respectfully. "I'm sorry to hear about his cousin Kim," the teenager said.

"His cousin Kim?" Kathryn asked suspiciously.

"Yes, the one who fell off the dock in Alaska and drowned."

"Oh, thank you," she replied, "but I'm afraid Brian's been telling you a tale. He doesn't *have* a cousin Kim."

Brian got this mischievous look on his face. It was hard to get angry at him when he was giving us such great entertainment.

Besides being a first-rate joke teller and yarn spinner, Brian was also an accomplished entrepreneur. He was always thinking up projects to do with his best friend, Ben. They would build a space go-cart, a racetrack, or a pollution detector. Once they built a high-tech mousetrap, and Brian begged us to let him stay up all night so he could witness the capture. He had a lemonade stand and produced a vaudeville show for the neighborhood kids—charging a small admission, of course. Brian organized pollution patrols at school and a neighborhood C.R.O.P. Walk to combat world hunger. Something was always happening when Brian was around.

He loved speaking in front of a crowd and often surprised me with how well he did. Brian had "stage presence" and a strong voice that carried clearly to the back rows. One summer when I was a camp doctor at a girls' summer camp, Brian decided to enter the talent contest. Later that evening, Kathryn and I sat in the audience, waiting for his turn. Brian went on stage and gave a short talk about karate (he had been taking lessons for nine months) and then started improvising a karate form. Something extraordinary happened as we watched him move around the stage, punching and kicking at imaginary foes, creating a dance that captivated us in its beauty. Kathryn and I looked at each other. "Wow!" we both said. Brian finished and took his bow, and the girls began clapping wildly. Then they started clapping and chanting in unison, "Bri-an, Bri-an, Bri-an!" This went on for several minutes. It was one of those magical moments.

Brian loved the comic strip *Calvin and Hobbes* and memorized all of our book collections. Sometimes, instead of telling a funny story, Brian would just recite the name of the book and the page number from memory, and we would look up the joke that Brian wanted us to read. Like Calvin, Brian had a "parents poll," and every few weeks, he would rate us on how we were doing. Sometimes I would be up (like when I helped Brian win the Cub Scout model car race) and Kathryn would be down, or vice versa. But, usually, we were somewhere in the middle. Brian and Calvin were so much alike, either entertaining us with their joy for life or struggling with its great mysteries.

Brian was a sweet, sensitive child. He was especially kind and loving to his sister, Lyn. Because of her handicaps, she had few friends. So Brian would play with her at school and protect her on the playground. When they were little, they loved sleeping together, and we would often find them in bed with their arms curled around each other. Brian had a special place in his heart for bigger girls, too. As he got older, he had a girlfriend named Jaimie, a bright and pretty little girl he had known since kindergarten. When he was six, Brian started writing poetry. One of his first poems was a Japanese haiku written for his karate instructor, who mounted it on the wall of the gym. He wrote one of my favorites for a school assignment when he was seven:

**Snake**
Snake slides, snake slithers
like wind over grass.
Safe from my tree
I watch him pass.

Every now and then, he would say or write something that would make me stop what I was doing. "Wow, that is *good*!" I would say. "I wish I could do that."

Our good friend, Clover, the mother of Brian's best friend, Ben, describes some of Brian's other special qualities.

Brian was an original, a little fireball who brought his own special brand of joy into the lives of all of us. He was gifted, witty, and wise beyond his years. What I most remember and treasure about Brian was the spontaneous, boundless, cosmic joy that he expressed so readily and awakened within me whenever he was around—a joy I had forgotten, or buried under the restrained customs of adulthood. Given the slightest provocation, this undiluted *joy* could come unstoppered in Brian with the power of a champagne cork. His supple little body would boogie down, and he would raise his voice that was at least twice the size and strength of his body in a cheer or a song of celebration, a song he had invented, a song that he flung from the bottom of his being to the highest heaven. Had I ever before heard a joy like that? No matter how seemingly heavy my cares and concerns, I couldn't help but be gay around Brian Korbon! He made us all laugh with his goofy jokes, his tall tales, his antics, and his plans.

"What would a bar be if it sold candy? ... A candy bar of course!"

"What do you get when you cross hot water and rabbits? …
Hot cross bunnies!"

Brian was a dreamer, an idealist, and perhaps it is lucky that
he never had to confront the pain of growing up. Yet, the magic
about him was that he was not your typical innocent child,
unaware of the world's evils. He seemed to have garnered all
the wisdom of disillusionment during his nine short years of
life, and yet in spite of that, he still could know and share that
joy I was telling you about.

Brian seemed to see and feel things more keenly than the rest of us,
and much of what he felt was painful. Because he was skinny and could
not run very fast, he was easy prey for the bullies at school. Though they
would often beat him up, Brian would not cower from them. Instead,
he made jokes and showed their weaknesses using his quick tongue,
saying things like: "His train of thought is waiting at the station" (a
quote from *Calvin and Hobbes*). Needless to say, it cost him. (He still
had bruises on his back from them when he died.) One time when he
was hurt and angry, he asked me, "Why do the strong hurt the weak
instead of helping them?"

Brian asked *all* the difficult questions, especially at bedtime.
Kathryn, a minister and pastoral counselor, tried her best to answer
them. But her answers always seemed to fall short, so she would hold
him, tell him how much she loved him, and help him say his prayers.
This comforted him enough to sleep. One day, we saw the movie *Ghost*,
and afterward, we talked about what might happen after death. That
night, as Kathryn was putting him to bed, Brian told her about the four
places you can go when you die. She only remembers two of them: you
can walk the earth or go to heaven. Looking back, she wishes that she
had paid more attention to what he was telling her.

## BRIAN BECOMES AFRAID

As Brian approached his ninth birthday, he became obsessed by
thoughts of death and kept insisting that he would not make it to
"double digits" (ten years old). He refused to celebrate his birthday,
saying it would bring his death closer. We reassured him that there was
no reason for him to worry about dying, but he became increasingly
upset and depressed. Brian talked about death at bedtime and was afraid

to sleep, becoming tired and despondent. We became so concerned that we took him to a child psychologist. Though we never discovered any new issues to deal with, Brian seemed to appreciate "Dr. Dan," and they both enjoyed their sessions together. Over the following months, they developed a warm friendship and slowly, with the help of teachers and friends, Brian became less fearful and had less trouble sleeping.

His ninth birthday, January 12, 1993, came, and—as Brian requested—we did not have a party to celebrate. It was a somber time, cheered up by Brian's unexpected appearance on national television. Months earlier, Brian learned that the TV show *America's Funniest People* was having tryouts at the local mall and insisted that we take him. We arrived at the mall and helped him register, along with hundreds of other people, and waited for his turn in front of the camera. They called Brian's name, and when he told his joke ("What do you call a Tyrannosaurus that is really scared? ... A nervous Rex."), the camera crew started laughing. They had him retape it five times.

The receptionist told us that perhaps one or two people from our area would appear on TV, and they would contact us if Brian made it. We never heard anything, so it was a surprise when Brian saw himself on Saturday morning's *America's Funniest Kids*, a spin-off of *America's Funniest People*. He came running into our bedroom, yelling, "Mom and Dad, I'm on TV!" It was good to see him happy.

The local newspaper and radio station did stories about his TV appearance, and then the following day, Brian was selected to be the guest ball boy at a University of Virginia basketball game. He got to meet all the players and was introduced to a sellout crowd, becoming a local celebrity. Brian always loved entertaining people, and now he was getting a chance to do it in a big way. "All it takes is a few lines in the paper and everyone wants your autograph!" he quipped.

A few months later, Brian's school principal sent a letter home telling us that Brian had been nominated for the gifted program. This came as a surprise since his grades were only average, and we never thought of him as academically gifted. But when the school gave us their questionnaire, it changed our understanding of Brian. It described him better than we could have. Humor, perfectionism, a strong sense of justice and spirituality, strong-willed, difficulty conforming—it was all pure Brian! Now we understood why he had such a hard time fitting in at school.

A few weeks before his death, Brian began to talk about taking a long trip—one day to Montana, another day to Wisconsin. He wrote to his grandparents, something that he had been meaning to do for a long time. Brian chose Kathryn's Mother's Day present weeks in advance, which he had never done before. Even more unusual, he insisted that Kathryn buy my Father's Day gift, though the holiday was months away. He even made peace with his bullies, the boys who were hard on him at school.

Then Lyn began drawing butterflies everywhere, and when she was not drawing them, she was asking us to write the word "butterfly" with her. Brian bought a box of glass butterflies at a toy store and painted them in beautiful, bright colors. Then, one day in late April, Brian decided that he would like to have a belated birthday celebration. He wanted a simple party with only a few friends and no presents. It would be a "Happy Spring Party," he announced. Brian invited his girlfriend, Jaimie; his best friend, Ben; and Cammie, a boy who had wanted to be friends with Brian. About this time, we noticed that our latest photograph of Brian was beginning to fade.

Two days before the party, Kathryn came home to find Brian sitting alongside the driveway with his covered wagon full of teddy bears, trying to build a fire. He told Kathryn that it was time for him to go on his trip. "I have to go. I have to go away," he said. Kathryn sat on the ground and then put Brian on her lap.

"But I'll miss you terribly if you go," she said.

"But I can't be afraid. I can't be a wimp. I have to go!" he answered.

Since the party was only two days away, she explained, it would be better if he delayed his trip, at least until after the party. She suggested another idea.

"Why don't we pitch the tent tomorrow and you can sleep out by yourself? That can be your trip for tomorrow," she offered.

This seemed like a great idea to him. So the next day, Brian, his teddy bears, and our dog, Sasha, camped out in the field next to our house—his first night alone in the dark. The next morning, he returned so proud of himself for staying out all night. We talked about his adventure over breakfast, and then we got the house ready for his party.

Brian's three guests arrived on the most beautiful spring morning you could imagine. The air was cool and sweet with the smell of honeysuckle. The clear blue sky was dotted with a few round, white clouds. We had a cake with candles, and Ben sang a song he had written for Brian ("Friends Forever, Always Together"). Cammie thanked Brian for inviting him, and in a quiet moment, Jaimie stole Brian away and gave him a secret kiss. They all played happily until their parents came to pick them up a few hours later. Brian said good-bye to his friends and went to his room to write some letters before his baseball game. Then, an hour later, I drove him to his game.

We stopped at the mailbox, and Brian put in two letters he had written but had not put stamps on. I said, "Brian, you know those won't get mailed without stamps."

But he looked me in the eye in his typical, determined fashion and said, "You don't understand; they *will* get there."

Rather than argue, I left the letters in the box, and we drove off to the baseball field. We talked about the upcoming game, and Brian told me how disappointed he was that he had not scored a run during his last game (he was left on third base and never got home). Today, he wanted to make it all the way home more than anything, he said.

We arrived at the field, and Brian bounded out of the car. I had never seen him so enthusiastic. He was the littlest kid on the team and not very good at baseball. He had always been afraid of the hardball—but not today! He begged Coach Parson to put him at second base instead of his usual position in right field, and during the warm-up, he charged after the ball without any fear. It was wonderful to see.

The game started, and I was cheering in the stands as Brian came up to bat. Being so little, he was walked to first base. The next batter hit a triple, and Brian tore around the bases, crossing home. Our eyes met as he trotted toward the sidelines, and he gave me a thumbs-up sign. He was beautiful. His eyes were shining—he was the happiest boy. We all cheered him as he ran by, giving high fives to everyone he passed, and then Brian disappeared into the dugout.

Later, they said that he just lay down on the bench and closed his eyes. "Yo! Brian!" they laughed. "Get up! Quit kidding around!" Then Brian rolled onto the ground, and they realized something was wrong. A few seconds later, Coach Parson carried Brian's limp body out of the dugout, and my happiness turned to horror. I ran to him and, fighting back my tears, started to resuscitate Brian. *His heart must have had a rhythm problem,* I thought. *We should be able to get him back.* But as I looked at his little blue face, something told me that Brian was not coming back. I have helped bring many people back from the edge of death, but I could sense that Brian's life was gone.

The rescue attempt went perfectly. The ambulance arrived in less than five minutes. Everyone did all the right things, but Brian's heart would not restart. I could not bring him back this time. We put Brian on a stretcher and continued to work on him in the ambulance during the short trip to the university hospital. The driver radioed ahead, and a medical team met us and whisked Brian into the emergency room. I followed and helped the anesthesiologist put a breathing tube into Brian's windpipe. Then, realizing I was not needed anymore, I quietly walked out into the hall and collapsed into a chair, weeping. I was no longer a physician—just a father grieving his dead son. I felt sick and empty and began to get weak.

In a few moments, I heard footsteps and looked up through my tears to see the distorted image of a nurse.

"Dr. Korbon, your wife is on the phone," she said.

"Oh … yes," I responded, trying to pull myself together. I rose and followed the nurse to the desk where I was handed a phone. Putting it to my ear, I heard Kathryn's voice.

"Gregg, what is happening? Is Brian okay?"

She was calling from her car on the way to the hospital. Kathryn and Lyn had come to meet us at the ball field, and one of the boys told them that Brian had been taken away in an ambulance. The boy said that Brian was sitting up, so Kathryn was not prepared for what I was about to tell her.

"Kath, I think Brian is gone." And as I heard myself say it, I began to sob again. Kathryn made a gasping sound.

"What?" she cried in anguish. "What?"

"His heart stopped beating, and I think we have lost him," I said through my sobs.

"I'm coming!" she answered. A few minutes later, Kathryn arrived, saying that a friend had taken Lyn to our home. A nurse took us into a little room where we waited for the next forty-five minutes as the medical team tried everything to save Brian. But it was futile, and we knew it.

Then another nurse led us into another room where we saw Brian's dead body lying on a table. *Though* I tried to brace myself, the sight of him sent shock waves of alarm throughout my body. *This can't be Brian,* I thought. *He is too pale and too still. Something is very wrong here!* But as I sat down next to him and felt the coldness of his skin, the reality of his death began to seep into me. Kathryn came closer, and then we took Brian's cold, limp hands in ours and wept as we told him how much we loved him. I had never felt so completely present as I did in that moment. Any thoughts I had of the past or future lay dead on the table with Brian's body. Minutes passed, and then our minister and several friends arrived and gave us support. After a while, our tears ran their course ... we hugged Brian's body and gently kissed him good-bye.

## OUR STRUGGLE TO UNDERSTAND

One of my friends from the hospital, Doug, drove me back to the baseball field so I could pick up my car. For some reason, it seemed important for me not to leave it alone overnight. We arrived at the field, and I got out of Doug's car. Even in my pain and grief, I realized that it was the most beautiful spring day I had ever seen. Cheers from a Little League game blended with the sounds of a nearby square dance. A cool breeze carried the smell of barbecue mixed with honeysuckle.

I reached up to wipe a tear from my eye, and the sour smell of Brian's vomit on my hands blended with the sweet smell of the honeysuckle. At that moment, my vision became clear and the colors, sounds, and smells became stronger and brighter than I had ever experienced—and I knew that I was at the center of life. The worst thing that I could imagine had just happened, and yet, I felt at peace. Everything was as it should be. Brian had died a happy boy. He had conquered his fears, which is more than most of us do. In my heart, I knew that if I could bring him back, it would be for me—not for him. Brian had finished his work here.

After a few minutes, Doug drove to my home with me following behind, barely able to drive. Many of our friends had already heard about Brian's death and were waiting for us by the time we arrived. As we went inside, the first things we saw were Brian's parent polls that he had left for us to find. Today, for the first time, he had given us his highest rating, a perfect two thousand.

More friends came throughout the day and night to help and comfort us, and we were grateful because we were in shock. Kathryn and I felt sick to our stomachs, weak, and like we were in a dream. It was good to have friends and family around to help us stay grounded. Lyn was also having trouble understanding that Brian would never be coming home again. So, later that night as I tucked her into bed, I cuddled up with her, and I tried to explain what death meant. "Brian is in heaven and won't be coming back to us," I said.

"He take airplane?" she asked.

"No," I answered, "when you go to heaven, you leave your body like a butterfly leaves its cocoon, and then you can fly without an airplane."

"Oh," she replied sadly. "Brian gone. I sad. It dark." She gazed up toward the ceiling, and then her eyes focused and looked into mine. Her expression was serene and confident. "Brian see light!" she said.

I looked at her in wonder. We had never talked of such things. What could she see? Then I felt a humming sensation in my back and "saw" a powerful, rippling river of luminous energy waves that were carrying us along. Somehow, I knew that they had always been there, but I just could not see them before. A great force was at work, and I sensed that Brian was still part of it. I was stunned by the wonder of it and felt that my life was changing, though I could not have imagined the strange and magical journey that was in store for me.

The next day was Mother's Day. I gave Kathryn the presents Brian had gotten for her: a trophy that said "Superstar Mom" and the card Brian had made for her. On it, he had written a special Mother's Day poem:

> Kathy
>> Loving, caring, daring
>> Married
>> Mother of Brian
>> Lover of the color pink
>> Who feels the guinea pig will pee
>> Who needs me
>> Who fears mad dogs
>> Who gives love
>> Who would like to see volcanoes

Resident of my house
Korbon
Love,
Brian

Kathryn was touched and appreciated how thoughtful Brian had been on this difficult Mother's Day.

Several months earlier, I had scheduled this week as a vacation to spend time with my family—the first time in my life I had ever done this. *A strange coincidence,* I thought. During this time, I learned how someone could die from despair. Kathryn and I could not eat or sleep, and I lost six pounds in two days—mostly tears. We needed the support of our family and friends to keep us going.

The next day, hundreds of people came to the funeral home to share our loss with us. They formed a long line, and when they hugged me, I could see Brian's body in his casket over their shoulder. He was dressed in his Cub Scout uniform that always made him feel so proud. I knew that he was not living there anymore, but I silently spoke to him anyway. "So, this is your gift to me, Brian. All of my life I've been afraid to let people get close to me. Now your loss is so great that I cannot bear it alone. Look at me, Brian. I am learning to love all these people like I loved you. Aren't you proud of me, Son?"

I learned a lot about hugging in those days. I could close my eyes and tell who my doctor friends were by their hugs. They would put their arms around my shoulders, but they always held their bellies back, even if they were crying with me. I realized that I had always done that, too. I had always held myself away. The best hugs were when someone would put their belly right up against mine and we would sob together, our bellies jiggling up against each other's.

The morning of the funeral, I received another shock as I read the letter Kathryn had just written to read at the funeral service later that afternoon. It read:

Dear Brian,
I always loved watching your mind work—the great games you used to imagine and the way you remembered all the names and dates I used to forget. I loved the great compassion you felt for all things living. How you cried the night I killed

the moth because it had a right to live, too. The great tenderness you showed to things small and weak.

I loved watching you play with Lyn. Your hugs and gentleness warmed my heart. As painful as it was, I loved the way you would struggle with life.

"Why would people pollute the earth?"

"How can people hate each other enough to fight wars and kill?"

And your struggle with God: "Why does God let children suffer?"

You journeyed through life with the heart of a poet. It was not always easy to stay with you, as you struggled on your rocky path. But somehow, through the pain and the anger, I was usually able to find you, and hold you, and love you. And I have given you all the hugs and kisses that could fit into nine years.

After your death, I came home and found a sign that you had just written and taped on your bedroom door. It said, "Brian is on a trip. Do not worry about me."

And though my heart feels as if it will break, I will not worry, because I know that you are at home and that you are with God. One night you promised me that if you died first, you would wait for me in heaven. As much as I would like to, I cannot hurry the day I will be with you, but I long for it, because I love you still.

Love,
Mom

I ran downstairs to Brian's room and saw the sign that Kathryn had described: "Brian is on a trip. Do not worry about me." Brian often had some sort of sign up: "Keep Out—Brian's Room" or something of the sort. But this one was different. I stared in wonder. "He knew ... he really knew he was leaving us," I said out loud. There was so much that I did not understand.

Later, at Brian's funeral, the congregation gasped when Kathryn read about his sign. She inspired all of us with her strength and love. Many of Brian's friends had come with their parents. Brian's baseball team was there, and the Cub Scouts brought their color guard. Kathryn and her minister friends created a beautiful children's service with stories and songs that were as comforting for the grown-ups as they were for the kids. It was a celebration of Brian's life, sad but wonderful. Our friend, Clover, expressed many of our feelings.

> Instead of feeling cheated that Brian was taken away from us too soon, let us be grateful that we had the gift that was Brian for as long as we did. No one can ever replace Brian in our hearts—but his place is not empty. My prayer is that Brian's spirit—a spirit of joy, wild and indomitable enough to combat and defeat the most insidious evil—will shine on in each of us, and that we will remember to express that joy whenever the opportunity arises. There isn't enough of it. And whenever I see that highest, farthest star twinkling merrily down on us, I think that's probably Brian, still laughing!

At the end of the service, in a dramatic display that Brian would have loved, lightning and thunder shook the church. And later, just as Brian had foretold in the car, we delivered his two letters to his friends—though they had no stamps. More than I had ever experienced, everything was coming together: Brian's foretelling of his death, his belated birthday party that was really a going-away party, his final "parents poll," the gifts, the letters, and the sign he left for us. He was telling us that he loved us and that we did not need to worry about him. There was a wonderful harmony to Brian's passage.

It took a while for me to appreciate all that Brian had done. He struggled with the hardest things I know: pain, fear, and even the knowledge of his own death—and accepted them. The day he celebrated his birthday and celebrated being alive was the day he died. Brian's last day on earth was the most life-affirming day I could imagine.

Time passed as Kathryn, Lyn, and I tried to put our lives back together and cope with the emptiness in our hearts. Summer changed to fall as our old apple trees—which had never borne fruit—gave us the sweetest, most delicious red apples. The colors of the fall leaves were especially beautiful and vibrant. They reminded me of some words Brian had written:

*The orange leaves always catch my eye as they wave along with the red leaves. Their sparkling shines out to the world. Then it is fall I know.*

I miss so many things about him: playing catch, holding him, laughing at his jokes—but especially, I miss his words. They reveal a beauty all around us that Brian saw more clearly than I. There were so many things that I still had to teach him, I thought. They all seem unimportant now, compared to what he taught me: that death, like all of life here on earth, can be embraced fully—without fear. No father could be more proud of his son.

And when my own time comes and my death draws near, I will think of Brian and the boundless joy in his eyes as he ran home on that beautiful spring day. I will reach out for him and for all that lies beyond. I will think of Brian … and I will not be afraid.

# Part II

"But Pooh, that is impossible," said Christopher Robin,
"One can't do that!"
"Yes, Christopher Robin, you are correct," replied Pooh.
"One can't ... but *two* can."

—A. A. Milne

# Chapter 2
# Aftermath—The
# Mysteries Continue

IN THE MONTHS FOLLOWING Brian's death, many questions remained, and just surviving in the midst of the shock and pain was difficult. Kathryn and I discovered that each person deals differently with a great loss like ours. Part of us was missing, and it was a different part for each of us. Kathryn, Lyn, and I had difficulty sharing our thoughts about what had really happened those last few months before Brian's death. As a result, it would be over a year before many of the pieces of information came together and another year after that before we could begin to share our feelings about them.

Our shock lasted for weeks, as we kept asking, "Is our little boy really gone?" It all had a dreamlike quality. I was trying to understand what had happened by reading and asking questions, but Kathryn was coping in another way, and my questions only upset her. And when I tried talking to other people about the wondrous things that had happened around Brian's death, I also received a reaction I did not expect. They would often become uncomfortable and change the subject.

So, over time, I became more careful in my speech. I would only mention Brian if someone else started talking about spiritual mystery, the death of a loved one, or asked me how we were doing with our grieving. Even then, many people still did not want to hear Brian's story. I was at a medical meeting, for example, and found myself strolling back to my hotel after dinner with a physician from India. He told me how he had just lost his young wife to cancer, leaving him behind with several small children. After he told me about how she died and that he believed in reincarnation, I mentioned that I, too, had lost a loved one and shared a brief version of Brian's story. But he looked away and changed the subject. *Why didn't he want to hear my son's beautiful story?* I wondered. *Why doesn't everyone want to?* And so it was when a reporter from a wire service called to follow up on Brian's story. When I got to the part where Brian said he was going to die and left us a note, his voice became hesitant and skeptical. "Oh?" he said. "Thank you for your time." No follow-up questions. No investigation to confirm the facts. Just a story about a little boy who died unexpectedly in a Little League game. I felt puzzled. *Surely, someone besides me must want to learn from Brian.* He had died publicly. It seemed that his death should have meaning for others as well as for me. Something very remarkable had happened, and people should pay attention.

About this time, we received two letters from the people who had received Brian's corneas and could now see again because of Brian. They were very grateful, and Kathryn and I appreciated their contacting us. The Little League board of directors decided to name the ball field where Brian died after him and, a few months later, held a dedication ceremony there. All the children in the league attended, and our mayor dedicated that day as Brian Korbon Day. A plaque was installed at the field inscribed with words that Kathryn wrote:

### Brian Korbon Field

On May 8, 1993, Brian Korbon died suddenly in the south dugout after scoring the first run of his Little League career. This ball field is dedicated to his wisdom, faith, and courage. May those who play here share Brian's sense of fair play and joy of life, and those who cheer them find a greater sense of community and love for their children.

The parents and community had renovated the entire complex and even installed lights. What had been a dumpy old ball field was transformed into one of the nicest in the area, and the lights made it safer for the kids to play in the evening. The ceremony began, and I became tearful when one of the boys sang the national anthem. I knew him but never realized he had such an angelic voice. When it was my turn to speak, I tried to maintain my composure as I addressed the crowd:

> On behalf of my wife, Kathryn, Brian's sister, Lyn, and of course Brian, I would like to thank all of you for this great honor. It was a year ago last Saturday that I sat in the stands and watched Brian run around the bases, scoring the first run of his Little League career. He was as happy as a little boy can be. Then he trotted into the dugout, lay down on the bench, and when his heart stopped beating, he died. Many of the Little Leaguers who are here today were there and some were in the dugout next to him. I would like to tell you some of Brian's story so that when you see the words *wisdom, faith*, and *courage* on the plaque, you will understand what they mean. And maybe, many years from now, when the children who are here now are grown and bring their own children to play here, they will remember what a special place this is.

I briefly recounted some of Brian's story, and then I turned to all the children assembled in the outfield and spoke to them.

> I know you children are getting old enough that you are beginning to think that the magic you believed in when you were little is just fairy tales and tricks, that the only things that are real are what you can see and touch. Trust your feelings. There is magic all around us. We just needed someone with the wisdom, faith, and courage to help us see it, someone like Brian. This is Brian's gift to us.

Several of the children who had been most upset by Brian's death told me that the ceremony was helpful in resolving their feelings of loss. It was a time and place where they could say good-bye in a positive way. Our church planted an ash tree in Brian's memory (ash is the wood used for making baseball bats), and the Cub Scouts planted a tree at Brian's school. They also dedicated their annual model car race, the Pinewood Derby, to him. (Brian had won the pack's first derby a few months before he died.) All this helped us to say a loving good-bye.

The local public access TV channel taped the dedication ceremony and played it on the air several times. A few people in the community saw the ceremony on TV and told us they were touched by Brian's story. It might have been a patient of mine or a bank teller or a student, but the ministers, psychologists, and physicians—the people I expected to be most supportive—seemed uncomfortable talking about death. I realized that before Brian's death, I had been, too. But I had changed. This, I learned at The Compassionate Friends meetings, is common to parents who have lost a child.

## THE COMPASSIONATE FRIENDS

The first time I heard of The Compassionate Friends was in the emergency room when Brian died. A nurse gave us a brochure and explained that The Compassionate Friends (TCF) is an organization for families who have experienced the death of a child. It provides monthly meetings for companionship and support.

It would be several months before Kathryn and I recovered enough to discuss going to a TCF meeting. She said she was not ready to go yet, but I had so many questions and felt I needed to try to find some answers. So I decided to go by myself. The meeting was on the same night that I was on call for emergencies, and an urgent case had kept me in the operating room until 7:45 PM. The meeting was to start at 8:00 PM, so I quickly changed clothes, thinking I could get to the meeting that was being held in a nearby church. As I reached the outside door of the hospital, I heard myself paged: "Dr. Korbon, please call the emergency room."

*What rotten timing,* I thought, *this better be important!* I turned around and walked to the emergency room.

"Dr. Korbon," the nurse said, "it's a friend of yours. Her little boy broke his arm, and she was relieved that you would be taking care of him."

I reviewed the chart: *Michael M., age nine, mother's name is Betty.*

*Oh, yes.* I remembered. *Michael was a friend of Brian's at preschool. That was five years ago. I'm surprised his mother remembers me.*

I entered the room, and Betty was glad to see me. She seemed to be more upset than I would have expected. Michael was doing pretty well. His arm was in a splint, and he seemed comfortable. Something did not add up.

"Gregg, my husband, James, just got out of the hospital a few hours ago. The doctors said his chest pain was nothing serious, but I am still worried about him, and now this!" She explained how James had developed chest pain the day before and seemed to have a strange feeling of dread. He had undergone a battery of tests that were all normal, and the doctors had sent him home. Then Michael fell on his arm, and Betty was scrambling to take care of both of them. Things seemed to be falling apart.

"I understand how things can pile up all of a sudden," I replied truthfully.

After reassuring Betty and explaining what would be happening, I took mother and son into the operating room and induced Michael's anesthesia without difficulty. Then one of the nurses took Betty out to the waiting room. The surgery went smoothly, and I then reunited Betty with her drowsy son in the recovery room. About an hour later, when Michael was ready to go back to his room, I said good-bye.

On my way home, I thought, *I guess this was more important than my going to the TCF meeting.* Little did I know.

The next day I was at home when Betty called, very upset. She said that James had died suddenly at home of a ruptured aneurysm in his chest. After telling me more of the details, Betty said that she had been to Brian's memorial service and wanted to know if we could help her plan James's service. I tried to comfort Betty, and then put Kathryn on the phone since she had done most of the arrangements for Brian's funeral. They talked, and then Kathryn went over to Betty's house and helped her make the arrangements.

Later, when Kathryn returned, she said that, though Betty had lots of friends and relatives around, they did not seem to be helping much. I saw what she meant the next evening when I attended the visitation at the funeral home. Though there were many people in attendance, none seemed to be genuinely caring for Betty. I was surprised that this role fell to me. I was even more surprised that I was comfortable doing it. If someone were to describe me previously, it would be as socially awkward, intellectually distant, and very ill at ease at funerals. Yet, I talked with Betty for over an hour. Someone would say something to her for a few minutes, and then she would come back to me and talk some more. Betty wanted to know more about Brian's story and seemed to draw comfort from it.

James's funeral was the next day, and Kathryn attended since I was working. She said the same situation with friends and relatives happened again. We had hardly known this woman, and yet, we seemed to be giving her something she needed and could not get from her own community. Instead of my going to a TCF meeting alone to receive help, I had joined with Kathryn to help Betty. *I guess I became a compassionate friend,* I reflected. I was not used to being like this. I seemed to have changed.

I think Kathryn changed too because she decided to go with me to the next TCF meeting in early December. It was a special candlelight service that was simple and touching. About fifty candles were lit in memory of children who had died. More important, the families heard their children's names spoken out loud as the candles were lit. For some parents, this was the only time of the year when the world acknowledged that their children had existed and were still loved.

We started attending the meetings and continued for about a year, learning many things. Our first lesson was that the loss of a loved one is timeless—only the shock goes away. The love remains as strong and the loss as great, even after decades. This love is also beyond comparison. Parents of the dead businessman, dead cheerleader, or stillborn baby all grieved equally. We grieving parents also found ourselves changed in similar ways. Since we had all survived the same horror, the worst thing a parent can imagine—the death of their child—we could talk, listen, and be silent with each other on a deeper level than with most other people. And we had all learned how to talk to a grieving person. There were no feeble attempts at false gaiety or false sadness—no attempts to compare or minimize our loss ("at least he died quickly"). We had all been hurt by others' attempts to "fix" or contain the grief. But our grief wanted to remain unfixed and open.

We also learned the healing power of sharing our stories and expressing our feelings about them. We could do this because we could stand in each other's pain, knowing from experience that it would not destroy us. Quite the contrary, connected to our common pain was a common love for someone who was no longer in physical form. This drew us together despite differences in belief or life experience. We also discovered that all of us had lost our fear of death and, with it, our fear of each other. I also realized that Brian had made his passing as easy for us as he could. Unlike the parents of the little girl who drowned in the family swimming pool or the mother of the estranged son who killed himself, we did not have feelings of guilt. As we looked back on our own experience, we realized that Brian had tied up all his loose ends. He was ready to go. The only unfinished tasks were ours. Brian, it seemed, had left us the opportunity for a clear and perfect grief. "Well, Kath, I guess when you consider this group, we are pretty lucky," I joked darkly.

During my time working in intensive care units, I had never understood why some families could not face reality—keeping a brain-dead relative on life support when there was no hope for recovery. Now, after listening to the mother who kept her estranged, suicidal son on a ventilator for several months, I finally understood. In order to let them go, you must have them first. The families that kept their brain-dead relatives alive had been emotionally distant from them. Now we saw parents like these reliving their pain and separation, meeting after meeting, month after month, trying to heal their grief enough to finally let their children go.

We also learned that other parents had described unusual behaviors before their children's accidental deaths. It was sort of "hush-hush." No one mentioned anything until Kathryn and I told some of Brian's story at a meeting. Then, after we finished, the other parents began to tell of their own unusual experiences. The first time we did this, there were fifteen sets of parents at the meeting, of whom eight were living with their children when they died. Of these eight, four children had premonitions concerning their accidental deaths. One twelve-year-old boy, who died in a car accident, gave his mother a list of his life accomplishments the evening before his death and talked about what he wanted to achieve in the future.

One mother, who worked at my hospital, told us the story of her four-year-old daughter, Stephanie. She died on a playground slide at her daycare center when a ribbon caught around her neck and strangled her. This mother brought in the picture Stephanie had drawn twenty minutes before she died, showing her dead body in dark colors hanging by the neck. Off to the side is a drawing of her in bright colors putting on a yellow halo, with a yellow angel in the sky dropping more halos down to her. "Stephanie always said that she did not want to grow up and go to school like the other children," this woman said. "She was very special and artistic and loved everything with all her heart. Almost every day, she would tell me, 'Know what? I love you with a mad passion!'" Stephanie sounded a lot like Brian to me. I also noticed that the media's coverage of her death withheld any mention of Stephanie's picture, just as they had omitted Brian's foretelling of his death.

A year later, at another TCF meeting, the same thing happened again. I told Brian's story and then spent the next hour listening as the other parents told of their own paranormal experiences surrounding the deaths of their children. All they needed to share these amazing stories was a safe and sympathetic ear, something they had not found previously. "This 'magic' stuff is all around us, Kath," I said later. "But nobody wants to talk about it."

### THE DREAMS THAT COME

Another thing we grieving parents would sometimes talk about were our dreams, which were often surprisingly similar and seemed to fall into three types. The first are the "pain" dreams that come in the days following the child's death. My own version of this was my nightly attempts to resuscitate Brian, which always failed. Unlike the actual resuscitation attempt when I shut down my emotions, though, in my dreams, I felt everything intensely and would desperately cry out for help. When the help did not come, I collapsed into tears of helplessness, holding Brian's limp body in my arms. This went on for the first week after Brian's death and made me relive the pain I had denied at the time. That is what these dreams do—keep us in touch with our pain.

When someone gets stuck in this stage, it is called a "pathological grief reaction," and the risk factors for this are isolation and helplessness. Friends and family naturally prevent this problem when they surround the grieving person with care and allow them to express their pain. Later, the ritualized actions of prayer, meditation, journaling, and attending a support group (getting and giving service) are of help in moving through the grieving process. The idea is to express the pain in a calm, nurturing environment, allowing the love in the present to heal the trauma of the past (pain reveals and love heals). To paraphrase

Carl Jung, the most common cause of mental illness is an inability to express pain through appropriate suffering.

The second type of dream is more reassuring and comes after our shock and pain have subsided, usually after a few months. I call them the "I'm okay" dreams. In these, our loved ones appear to be content and well taken care of. If they died as children, they often appear older and more independent, and though we often want to hold on to them, they seem to prefer their freedom. The loved one's death appears to be much more of a hardship for us than it is for them. Sometimes, the dream will reveal useful information or give us guidance, but its primary message seems to be that our loved one is okay and we need not worry about them.

The last type of dream comes later, usually after several years. These are the "good-bye" dreams, and several I have heard went like this: you are driving a car and see your loved one standing alongside the road. Overjoyed, you pull over, and they get in with you. You visit together and then continue driving, but in a little while, they ask you to stop the car. You know, or they tell you, that it is time for them to go their separate way. Then they get out of the car, say good-bye, and disappear.

My own variation of this dream was that Brian (now a handsome young man with a beard) asked to be let out at a road that was still under construction. Later, after I drove to my destination, I returned to where I dropped Brian off and called for him to return. He dutifully appeared and got into the back seat of my car as I happily talked to him. But he started to expand and lose his human shape, obviously becoming uncomfortable as he was confined by the smallness of my car. I realized that I did not know what I was doing and apologized for holding on to him. Then Brian vanished from sight, though the feeling of love for him remained.

Each person's dream was a little different, reflecting his or her own unique experience. But as has been observed across many cultures and times, there were often remarkable patterns of similarity. Commonly, our dreams use symbols from everyday life—like driving a car (which, in my dream, represented my own life's journey). Occasionally, our dreams will show us symbols from ancient mythology, even if we have not seen them before. They may also use symbols from sacred geometry, like the vortex (or its two dimensional projection, the spiral)—which often represents a major life transformation. The mysterious intelligence of our dreams is unlimited, and the more we study them, the more they reveal.

## A SHARED DREAM

We did not look forward to our first Christmas without Brian, so it was with relief that we accepted Kathryn's parents' invitation to spend the holiday with them at a hotel in Hershey, Pennsylvania. (It helped me to know that if Brian could not be there, at least I could eat a lot of chocolate.) Kathryn, Lyn, and I drove up on a snowy Friday evening and joined my in-laws, who had already arrived. We had three adjoining rooms, where we unpacked our clothes and gifts. We went to dinner, and afterward, we went to bed early since we were all tired and a little sad.

The next morning, as we were opening presents, we were surprised to discover that Kathryn, my mother-in-law, and Lyn had all dreamt of Brian. (He always had a way with the ladies.) Brian came to each of them and said that he was happy and not to worry about him. When the dream ended, everyone woke up and noted the time to be 2:00 AM. We appreciated Brian's thoughtfulness and felt that he had given us the best Christmas present he could. This made us feel better, and we enjoyed the rest of the weekend together.

As time went on, there were a lot of other painful "firsts" without Brian: the first New Year's Day, the first end of summer camp as we saw the families reuniting and heading home, the first day of school, and many other events that we did not see coming until they were upon us. Our loneliest times were often when we came back from a trip and realized that our home felt empty without Brian.

Over the next several months, I tried to slowly rebuild my life. It took me three months before I could give anesthesia to children again, and even then it was a struggle. When I placed the oxygen mask over their beautiful young faces, I had to concentrate—trying not to flash back to Brian's resuscitation scene. Sometimes, though, I would remember the whiteness of Brian's skin and the blueness of his lips. Then, at the end of the day, I would cry as I drove home. Gradually, the pain of these experiences lessened.

Occasionally, someone would ask me why I was taking Brian's death so well. Sometimes they asked why some people become bitter and isolated after the death of a loved one, while I seemed to be warmer and more open. I did not know how to answer this. All I knew was that I was grateful for the clarity Brian had shown me. There was no doubt in my mind that Brian had finished his life and opened up new possibilities for mine.

"If you are thirsty, the river comes to you,
if you are not, the river does not exist."

—Sat Prem

# Chapter 3
# Further Evidence for an Invisible World

WHAT DO YOU DO when your own experiences should be impossible according to everything you were taught? How can a child know the future? How can people share a common dream? And what of the rippling river of energy waves I saw with Lyn the night Brian died—what was that all about? I did not know, but the one thing I did know was that my old belief system was shattered. There was, obviously, more to reality than I knew, and I wanted to understand what had happened. But before I go into this, I think it would be helpful to tell you a little more about what was happening to me around the time Brian died.

If you met me at a cocktail party, you probably would not be impressed. I am soft-spoken, slightly built, and shy. However, though my social skills are limited, I always found that the one place I could be successful was in school. So I stayed in academics for many years, graduating from Duke University in three years with an A- average, then going on to Duke University School of Medicine, and later, teaching there as well as at the University of Virginia. At the time, Virginia had one of the premier pain programs in the country. Pain management is my subspecialty along with epidurals and other types of nerve blocks.

By the time Brian was three and getting over most of his medical problems, my academic career was taking off. I was making a name for myself and receiving job offers to direct the pain programs at some of the most prestigious hospitals in the country. But something felt wrong with my work, and I did not want to become like the academicians I saw around me. You see, because I was uncomfortable with people, I had retreated into the ivory tower of cool, academic intellectualization. And, by rights, I should have fit right in—but I did not. Something was missing, though I did not know what. I could only see that my life wanted to follow another path. So I quit academics and entered private practice at our community hospital, which allowed me to rediscover my enjoyment of patient care and gave me more time to spend with my family.

My marriage had been strained for many years by all of Brian's and Lyn's medical problems, and Kathryn and I had been in survival mode ever since. During our courtship, I was attracted to Kathryn's good looks, her spunk, and her sociability. But years of stress and lack of sleep had taken their toll; her spunkiness was gone, and we were too exhausted to have a social life. So, now that I was no longer working eighty hours a week, I could spend more of my time at home helping Kathryn and the kids. I had hoped things would get better, and for a year and a half, they did—a little. Brian was finished with his surgeries, and Lyn was sleeping better. But both children still required lots of care—Lyn for her disabilities and Brian for his giftedness and inability to fit in to normal public school life. Brian was getting ready to leave us, though we did not believe him when he told us, and this gave our family life an eerie feeling.

Then, after Brian died, the emptiness in our life was huge. Friends and relatives were helpful, but after a while, the casserole dishes stopped coming, and we had to get by on our own. Something was missing from all of us. Some of it was different for each of us, and none of us could fill each other's empty place. For me, the emptiness became a clear place in my mind, and, as someone most comfortable in the world of ideas, this is where I began my search for understanding.

Now, having said this, I will return to where I was when I first began to explore the mystery that Brian left for me. And if my discussion starts off a little too intellectual—too reflective, cool, and hollow for your liking—I understand. But, at the time, this was the best way I knew of dealing with the loss of my son—as I will explain later.

## THE SEARCH FOR UNDERSTANDING

As I recovered from the shock of Brian's death, I looked for answers to the questions he left behind. I read everything I could find dealing with death and dying, near-death experience, pre-death experience, religion, science, philosophy, psychology, and parapsychology. I read more books in two years than in the previous twenty, gathering information and stories that began to form a pattern. My grief seemed to be part of a larger process that took me to the very roots of my being, revealing a strange beauty that I later recognized in the writings of poets and mystics. During this period, I also watched myself change from a closed-minded, church-going agnostic to someone who could no longer say anything was impossible.

The more I searched, the more I found that there *was* information available concerning other realities and other ways of thinking. Much of it, however, has been kept out of scientific journals and the media, like the mystical parts of Brian's story had been. For example, I often found several good studies published in obscure journals showing a consistent paranormal effect, and a single study of poor quality discrediting the effect. And this one poor study would be published in a prestigious journal and broadcast by the media. There is, obviously, a strong denial of paranormal experiences in our culture, and this, I think, is why so many people did not want to hear Brian's story. They could not accept the truth of it without doubting their own beliefs—their own worldviews.

## DEATH AND DYING—OTHER PEOPLE'S EXPERIENCES

The experiences surrounding Brian's death were not as unique as I had first thought. Many other people described similar occurrences. Brian's story was unusual in that our experiences painted a more complete picture of an interaction with an invisible world. Many other children had predicted their unexpected deaths; a few had left notes, and some had described what happens after death. Other parents described experiences of connection with their recently dead children, vivid sensations and feelings of clarity and peace. Some others had described the vibration I felt, as well as the sensation of being carried along by waves of energy. Siblings reported seeing their dead brother or sister in the "light." But I could not find any report that described everything we had experienced with Brian, just one or two of the unusual features. All the same, it was comforting to know that others had similar experiences.

## THE SCIENCE OF PRAYER

Dr. Larry Dossey's book, *Healing Words*, reviews the hundreds of scientific studies done on the effects of prayer upon living organisms. It shows that, in most cases, prayer works, even on plants and bacteria. If you pray for one group of seeds to grow more than another, for example, it usually does. One of the most powerful influences on the effect of the prayer is the amount of love the people feel when they are praying. If they feel a particularly strong connection to the object of the prayer, the effect of the prayer increases.

These experiments seemed simple enough that I tried one with my family, and the results were remarkable. We planted forty marigold seeds (they were Brian's favorite flower) in a seed tray, covered them with a clear plastic top, and prayed for half of them. After one week, we uncovered the tray and found sixteen healthy plants in the prayer side, and only three sickly ones in the other side. Our results were much more dramatic than usually reported in studies. (Typically, you cannot see much difference and need statistical analysis to reveal an effect.) These results and all the other unusual occurrences I am describing were not reasonable—but they happened anyway.

## RECEIVING INFORMATION—REMOTE VIEWING

Remote viewing is receiving visual information during meditation (commonly called "clairvoyance") under scientifically controlled conditions. Experiments at Duke, and more recently Stanford and Princeton, have shown that subjects selected for this talent can view places in their minds that they have never physically seen. When given a sealed envelope containing a picture or coordinates of a location, remote viewers can draw pictures and provide other information about the location, often with great detail, and their accuracy has been shown to be much greater than would be predicted by chance.

One of these individuals, Joe McMoneagle, is a retired military intelligence officer who has been studied by scientists for over twenty years (making him one of the most verified psychics in history). When guessing which of four pictures are in a sealed envelope, he is correct 47 percent of the time (chance being correct 25 percent of the time), and 23 percent of the time he can draw an almost exact duplicate of the picture in the envelope. Interestingly, Joe reports that he can guess the correct picture 100 percent of the time when remote viewing nuclear facilities. Joe's accuracy is as good as any remote viewer in the world, and in the last several years, he has demonstrated his abilities on national television in the United States, Great Britain, and Japan. Under controlled conditions, Joe was highly accurate in almost all television trials, drawing detailed pictures of places he had no physical way of seeing.

Joe is a friend of mine, and when I asked him what was going on, he replied that the unconscious has access to *all* information and is not limited by space or time. When one clears the mind and asks for information, it appears in visions, symbols, and instances of "knowing." The big problem, Joe says, is that his mind tries to take control and recreate known patterns from the past. Joe has improved his accuracy by finding ways to clear his thoughts, allowing the new information from the unconscious to flow into the present.

Inspired by Joe, I decided to try remote viewing myself at a weeklong workshop called "Remote Viewing Practicum" at The Monroe Institute (more about this place later). A former army intelligence officer, Skip Atwater, taught the workshop. Skip had originated the military's first remote-viewing program and had recruited Joe McMoneagle into it. Then, over the years—improvising along the way—Skip helped Joe develop his amazing accuracy. With all this experience to guide us, by the end of the workshop, our group of twelve students guessed the correct picture 52 percent of the time—with a few almost perfect drawings of the picture in the envelope, but we were not as good as Joe in this respect.

One of the final exercises involved a remote viewing of a "hard object" (an actual object concealed in a brown paper bag) one hour *before* the target was selected. We worked in teams, drawing and describing the target. Then we went into a room with brown paper bags on a table, numbered one through six. A single die was rolled to determine the target, and the corresponding bag was opened to reveal the object. Our accuracy in this exercise was just as good as with the ones we had previously done in real time—with one of us, a meditation teacher from Japan, drawing a perfect replica of the red spool of thread that was in the bag, complete with the label markings on one end. So,

I can tell you from my own experiences that under special conditions, it really *is* possible to see the future.

## SHARED THOUGHTS—TELEPATHY

Biologist Rupert Sheldrake has observed that dogs, under randomized, controlled conditions, exhibit behavior anticipating their masters' returning home (excitedly looking out the window). Sheldrake also documents that a parrot raised by a linguist to use language equivalent to a three-year-old child, under controlled conditions, describes what its owner is thinking or even dreaming while asleep.

My own experience with animals also suggests a telepathic ability. When I worked at a dude ranch, for example, I noticed that the horses in a distant pasture seemed to know what we were planning. If we were just bringing them feed, they would be waiting at the gate as we drove up in our truck. But if we were also planning to rope one of them to give a medical treatment that they obviously did not like, they would be on the other side of the field as we drove up. When I asked the owner of the ranch about this, he said that they always seemed to know what we were thinking.

Another example of animal telepathy was our dog, Sasha, who always disappeared whenever we planned to give her a bath, which she hated. She also hated our neighbor who lived out of sight a half mile away (a fellow who, on several occasions, threatened to shoot Sasha with the .357 Magnum he often carried). His daughter, who was friendly and lived between his house and ours, told us that Sasha would start barking the moment her father opened his door to walk out to our property boundary. But Sasha would not bark the many other times her father left his house.

One of my own early experiences of human telepathy occurred during a shamanic meditation workshop I attended, also at The Monroe Institute. There were twenty-two of us in the room—only two of whom I had met casually. The leader was teaching a Native American Indian practice that uses a visualization of entering the earth, seeking a teacher, and then asking for information. He asked if anyone had a problem for which they wanted help. I raised my hand, and he instructed me to silently think of my problem while the other people in the room entered a state of meditation and asked for words of help for me.

I silently asked for advice on what to do about my daughter, Lyn. She was constantly providing challenges at home and school, and we were often struggling with them. At the end of the meditation, everyone silently wrote down the information they received and gave me their papers as they left the room. Though no one knew my question, or even that I had a handicapped daughter, these are some of the answers I was given. My comments are in brackets.

1. Concerning daughter: more love and also sense of deeper peace because she is special … But she comes with a great gift to bring (like others of her kind) a special note or resonance of gentle light to the earth.
2. Try Edgar Cayce's castor oil packs to your daughter's abdomen. [Edgar Cayce was a famous psychic and healer in the early twentieth century and recommended castor oil packs for children with neurological problems.]
3. She is supposed to use castor oil packs to help the immunity. Go to an osteopath for adjustments [another Cayce recommendation for neurological problems].
4. Tell her stories.
5. Use crystals. Healer in Tennessee. The healing will come through your own hands—there may be a crystal involved.

These responses to my silent question seemed to reveal a connection between our thoughts that was more than I would have expected from chance alone.

### ANCIENT MYSTERIES

Some things our early ancestors did continue to baffle us. For example, how did they move huge, multiton stone blocks from a quarry in a valley to a high mountaintop many miles away and thousands of feet up steep, rugged slopes at religious sites like Machu Picchu, Peru? How did ancient Egyptians from about 10,000 BCE place stones in the desert showing the precise position and *distance* to the stars in the belt of the constellation Orion? Their distance accuracy rivals our best satellite technology, and the stones' placements indicate that our ancestors knew the twenty-six-thousand-year cycle of the stars' motion through the heavens.

Cave paintings dating back as far as forty thousand years ago show scenes from ancient people's lives, as well as symbols of a more spiritual nature: waves, spirals, crosses, etc. A few years ago, on a trip to Arizona, Kathryn and I visited an ancient Native American cliff dwelling with many different wall paintings and lots of waves and spirals, including one that looked like this:

When Kathryn saw it, she whispered to me, "That's it! That is the shape I saw in my mind when Brian died!" When we asked our archeologist guide what it meant, he answered that this symbol represents disaster. The smooth curve of the spiral, symbolizing continuous change, straightens for a while but then makes sharp changes of direction, representing intermittent and traumatic change. This symbol obviously came from deep in the unconscious and joined the mind of Kathryn to others who felt a loss as great as hers. Perhaps the person who painted the symbol a thousand years ago was a mother who lost a beautiful and gifted child and grieved with all her heart, as Kathryn did. Regardless of the specific reality, they shared a heart connection that transcended the limits of space and time.

### SHARED FEELINGS—THE HEART CONNECTION

I never had any luck finding four-leaf clovers. No matter how hard I looked, I had never found one by myself. So it was with interest that I read in Andrew Weil's book, *Spontaneous Healing*, that he had the same problem until he spent time with a friend who had the knack. Searching for clovers with his friend seemed to break the spell, and now Dr. Weil can find four-leaf clovers on his own. A few days after reading this, I found myself in my backyard with a young woman named Jackie, who was visiting us. She started looking down into the grass, walking around as she told me this story.

> When I was a little girl, I had such low self-esteem that I was always looking down. One thing it made me good at was finding four-leaf clovers, sometimes even five-leaf ones. I went to a Catholic school, and the mother superior was very kind to me, so I gave her a four-leaf clover I had found. For the rest of my years there, she always called me her "four-leaf clover girl."

Moments later, Jackie bent over, picked up something from the grass, and handed it to me. It was a four-leaf clover, and as she gave it to me, I felt a warmth in my heart that told me she was also giving me something else, a part of herself.

The next day, I was playing with my daughter in the same yard when it occurred to me that maybe now, the spell might be broken for me. I started looking into the grass and felt a warmth in my heart. I knew what my eyes were going to find—a five-leaf clover—and it seemed completely natural that it was there. I felt a sense of peace, love, and harmony—and since then, I have been able to find four-leaf clovers like my friend Jackie.

## SAVANTS

There are people who have profound mental disabilities but possess a single area of profound ability. Psychiatrist Darold Treffert catalogs many of their talents in his book, *Extraordinary People*. The character, Raymond, in the movie *Rain Man* (based on real-life savant, Kim Peek) is an example of what they can do. Somehow, these people "know" things beyond any reasonable explanation. Identical twins with IQs of 25 (someone with an IQ of 50 is severely retarded) can each, instantly, tell you the day of the week, the fullness of the moon, and the level of the tides for any date forty thousand years in the past or the future. In 1752, Europe changed from the Julian to the Gregorian calendar, and the twins will change calendars appropriately at that date, even though they have no understanding of history, no knowledge of calendar systems, and cannot add the simplest numbers.

One savant, blind from birth, can run through the woods without tripping or running into anything. Currently, Daniel Tammet, a savant with only mild autism (Asperger's syndrome), is giving scientists an insight into his ability. Daniel can perform extremely difficult calculations in his head by "seeing" the numbers appear to him, one piece at a time. Rather than using reason, Daniel seems to be using an intuitive or artistic process. The film, *Brainman*, documents his abilities, and Daniel's book, *Born on a Blue Day*, further describes his amazing gifts.

## THE MYSTERIES OF SCIENCE

Scientists have discovered that what we perceive as reality is only a small part of the complete universe. Most of the universe is made up of "dark energy" which exists in "empty" space—the cold, dark space devoid of all known energy and matter. This dark energy is incredibly powerful, causing the universe to expand and giving it a certain direction. What else does this unseen field of energy do? All we know is that it influences and connects our known reality in ways that we do not understand.

Regarding this mysterious connection, whenever two subatomic particles come into contact, their waves come into resonance, and they "mate" for the rest of their lives. Then, if you separate them to the far ends of the universe and change the spin of one, the other will change its spin at exactly the same instant—what Einstein called "spooky action at a distance." When humans fall in love or a mother nurses her baby, the strong electromagnetic waves of their hearts also come into resonance. This harmonic condition, much like a wireless broadband connection, is associated with many extraordinary events such as mothers lifting cars off of their injured children or parents waking up in the middle of the night knowing that their children, far from home, have been injured. Love (resonance) seems to provide a mysterious connection for both subatomic particles and humans, and allows them to do the unexpected.

Is the universe intelligent? Here is the evidence so far: Since all of the various constants in nature (gravity; speed of light; the weight, charge, and spin of subatomic particles) are interrelated and if any one constant were slightly different, life—as we know it—could not exist. The probability of this happening by chance is infinitely small and, therefore, beyond common reason. Also, when scientists perform experiments with subatomic matter, it always takes the appropriate form (wave or particle) to satisfy what the scientist wants to measure. If matter is observed during the experiment, it acts like a particle; if not, it acts like a wave. So, even the smallest particles of matter seem to "know" that they are being observed.

In between the huge universe and the tiny subatomic world (exactly in the middle, in fact), we have our own planet, with little organisms like bacteria and big ones like humans. So, which is smarter? Well, humans take years to develop a new antibiotic, but bacteria can change their structure and function to defeat the drug in only weeks (maybe because bacteria don't have as many meetings), and these new, drug-resistant bacteria often pop up in different parts of the world at the same time. Individually, bacteria act stupid, but taken as a collective whole, they are smart. In fact, in this ongoing battle of wits between people and bugs, most scientists are betting on the bugs.

## THE CREATIVE MIND

As interesting and mysterious as modern science is, there is something else that I find equally fascinating, the minds of the great artists and scientists and the creative process that led them to their breakthroughs.

When I was learning about scientific discoveries in college, I could usually see how most of them followed logically from the science of their time. There were exceptions, though—usually the great leaps of genius—like general relativity (the idea that gravity is caused by the curving of space/time). It did not follow from anything I could see. How had Einstein come up with it? There was nothing in our physics textbooks to tell us. It was only as I began reading the mystical literature that I found descriptions of what had happened, and it began to sound familiar.

What we call "genius" does not occur by logic, or what we call "reason." It comes as "vision," and it does not come when the scientist is trying but, rather, while relaxing or even dreaming. The great scientists have this one thing in common—"vision." As Einstein put it, "the most beautiful and most profound emotion we can experience is the sensation of the mystical. It is the sower of all true science." Max

Planck, the father of quantum theory, said, "It is surely no accident that precisely the greatest thinkers of all times were also deeply religious." Einstein got E=MC² and his new ideas about gravity while in a dream state. He got the vision first and then spent years writing the equations to prove it. Similarly, Mozart, Mendelssohn, and Bach "heard" an entire musical piece in a momentary flash of inspiration, and then labored to write it down. As Bill Monroe, the father of bluegrass music, said, "I ain't never wrote nothin'! Them songs was float'n in the air, and I just pulled 'em down." Similarly, artists have visions of new concepts, decades before scientists describe them in technical terms. For example, Van Gogh painted matter waves before de Broglie wrote the equations, Jackson Pollock painted fractal geometry before Mandlebrot described the mathematics, and Dali painted a fourth-dimensional hypercube before scientists found it useful. Just as Joe McMoneagle can "see" places he has never physically seen, creative vision lies in the quiet, open mind.

"Nothing you love is lost. Not really. Things, people—they always go away, sooner or later. You can't hold them, any more than you can hold moonlight. But if they've touched you, if they're inside you, then they're still yours. The only things you ever really have are the ones you hold inside your heart."

—Bruce Coville, *Jeremy Thatcher, Dragon Hatcher*
(One of Brian's favorite books)

# Chapter 4
# Magical Journey

THOUGH MODERN SCIENCE IS difficult to understand, it is quite useful. All of our lasers, DVDs, transistors, and computer chips; fully one-third of our economy depends upon its strange behavior. Tunneling electron microscopes use a particle's "ghostlike" ability to skip in and out of physical reality to give us pictures of molecules. Star Trek–like teleportation chambers use "spooky action at a distance" to instantly transfer particles across space. And quantum computers use resources outside the boundaries of space and time to outperform traditional computers. The key concept underlying all of this science is that there are, indeed, two worlds: the physical one we can see and touch and the nonphysical one we cannot. The reason I emphasize this idea of two worlds again is because, since Brian's death, I have found myself with a foot in both of them.

Survivors of near-death experiences often report that they have glimpses of the future and other people's thoughts, experience an increased number of meaningful coincidences (synchronicities), and sense greater connection with all things. It seems that Brian has been my own near-death experience because, since he died, these things have been happening to me, too. The experiences described in the previous chapter—remote viewing, effects of prayer, sharing thoughts and feelings—are only a small part of the changes that have occurred in my life. And it was not a conscious process (on my part at least), because I never believed that such things were possible. But they happened anyway, and much of the story begins on a hot, desolate racetrack in central Florida.

## AROUND AND AROUND

About a year after Brian died (as I was finishing the first chapter of this book), a good friend of mine, Chris, invited me to go with him to race-car driving school at Sebring, Florida. It so happened that this was the one remaining thing I had dreamed of doing as a child but had not yet done. The desire to try racing had been fading, but I thought it would be fun to spend time with Chris, and last dreams die hard. So we ended up going down to Florida twice over the next year, and it was an interesting and educational experience for several reasons.

For one thing, Chris and I, as physicians, felt like the working poor. The other eight men in the class, all in their thirties, were almost all independently wealthy. One was a world champion athlete, most had raced before, and many owned their own racing cars. One corporate raider flew in on his private jet. Another driver, a wealthy South American playboy, kept wrecking and paying for his race cars—buying three cars in six days. Of all the sports I had tried, this was definitely the most expensive.

I had thought that race-car driving would be glamorous, but, surprisingly, it was just the opposite. Most racetracks, I learned, are in the middle of nowhere, and Sebring was no exception. It is a desolate, World War II airfield in central Florida, a two-hour drive from Orlando. There were two restaurants and one motel recommended in the area, and Chris and I would often see the other drivers eating dinner alone at separate tables. Although they were friendly, there was never any invitation to join them, which was okay with us since we were having a good time by ourselves. I noticed that most of the drivers were single, and the few girlfriends who came along stayed apart from each other as well. It was a solitary group to be sure and a quiet one, too. Some of this may have been from the pressure of the course, which was very intense. But I had been through enough challenges in the military and elsewhere to appreciate that this group was unusually quiet.

The psychology of driving was interesting, also. There is a line of maximum speed around a racecourse, and the driver's job is to drive it as fast as possible without losing control. The driver who can push his car to the edge the longest is the fastest. The tires should always be squealing on the turns. You accelerate as fast as you can and then, at the next corner, stand on the brakes while double-clutch down-shifting (not easy with size twelve feet), squealing the tires and leaving rubber marks but never quite locking the wheels completely. Besides driving to the limit, the challenging part is finding the optimum line, which is always changing due to temperature, track conditions, and the other drivers' positions.

On a typical day, we would alternate driving and classroom lessons for eight hours and by day's end would have used up one set of tires, a lot of gasoline, and, for me, a lot of brain energy. Since I was a beginner, it was as mentally exhausting as anything I had done, and driving to the airport after our first course, Chris and I could not think clearly. We had trouble concentrating, missed our turnoff, and at the airport, I forgot to notice the end of the moving sidewalk and fell over, bags and all, into a giddy, laughing heap.

The main thing that I learned at driving school was not how to drive faster, although I did do that. It was why we were all there. Here were resourceful, talented men in their prime who got into cars and drove around and around in frantic, adrenaline-soaked circles—around and around again, using up all their available energy—then always returning to the same place again as they pulled into the pit. It was almost a caricature of how I had spent my life before Brian died—running unconsciously from activity to activity, running away from the emptiness that I felt within myself. My desperation had been so great that I had pushed myself to within a whisper of death several times—always because I could not consciously face my own emptiness.

When I was growing up as an only child in Chicago, my life was very chaotic. My parents divorced, and we moved every year or two. So, I was usually without a father, friends, or community, and to fill this void, I turned to the heroes of my time for role models: Superman, Batman, and James Bond. *If only,* I thought, *I could be powerful like they are; I would feel happy and complete.*

So I tried to master everything I thought would give me power. I learned to fight, learned to swim down sixty feet underwater on a single breath, learned to fly airplanes in simulated air combat and pull six Gs without blacking out. I jumped out of airplanes and skydived six thousand feet before pulling my parachute. I pushed every limit I could find, only to return, inevitably, back to the same place—the pit of my emptiness. I had mastered every challenge, and I was as empty and incomplete as ever. I had found no real power in all my exploits, no matter how heroic I had tried to make them. My emptiness had been offering itself to explore and heal, but I had chosen to run rather than accept its dark offering. Now, when I looked around the racetrack, I saw what I had not seen before. The other men were in the throes of their own inner conflicts, and like me before, they were not aware of it—they were in unconscious flight. Because my illusions were beginning to lift, I could see it more clearly. We were seeking momentary distraction and the illusion of power. Yes, it was a joy to drive a well-designed machine to its limit, but not enough to leave my family and spend my hard-earned money. I could get the same challenge at home riding my bicycle. No, for me, it was a final look back at the way I had spent most of my life—in unconscious flight.

I see now that the heroes of my boyhood are really characters born from emptiness and pain. They are all suffering a lost love and holding on to an unresolved grief. As a result, they go to pieces, creating split identities—one meek and secret, the other bold and violent—each expressing its pain behind a different kind of mask. And because they hide their true selves and true emotions, they are emotionally distant and alone. Realizing this, I did not want to be like them anymore. I did not want their masks, conflict, or separation. Instead, I just wanted to explore my own emptiness and pain—the denial of which had been driving my own life in frantic circles.

## BEYOND THE RACETRACK—THE MONROE INSTITUTE

Just after returning from my second and last trip to Sebring, I was eating lunch in the hospital cafeteria with a friend, Faye, the director of our cancer center. I was telling her about my trip and how I felt like it was closing a chapter of my life. "Now that I have done everything that I wanted as a child," I said, "I wonder what is in store for me next?"

Faye did not respond to my question directly but, instead, started talking about a job she had had several years before. She had worked as a part-time secretary for the president of the local cable TV company in town. The man's name was Robert Monroe, and he was an interesting person, as it turned out. It became apparent, Faye said, that many of his activities were not limited to the cable TV business. She received phone messages for him relating to several books he had written about "strange sorts of things—out-of-body experiences and altered states of consciousness" (whatever that meant). Still, she said he seemed like a nice older man and was on good terms with one of his ex-wives, which she took as a good sign. After a few minutes, the topic of conversation changed, and I took little note of it at the time.

A few weeks later, I decided to begin riding my bicycle to work. I had thought about doing this before Brian died, but everyone told me it was too dangerous. The roads were poorly designed for bicycles: high-speed traffic, no shoulders, blind curves, and every year, a bicyclist or two would get killed by cars. But dying no longer frightened me, so I thought I would try bike commuting for a year and see if I liked it. I wanted to learn how to maintain and repair my bike, and the best bicycle mechanic in town, I was told repeatedly, was a fellow named Scott. So I enrolled in one of his evening courses. (I was the only student over the age of twelve and also the only bald one.)

Scott and I became friends, and he invited me to his house the next Sunday morning to go mountain biking with some kids he invited over regularly. Scott and his wife had an alternative lifestyle and lived simply in a cabin they built by themselves far out in the country. They homeschooled their children, and I learned that the homeschoolers had their own social community. These were the children with whom I would be riding. Scott commuted to town by bicycle thirty-two miles each way on steep, backcountry roads in all kinds of weather. He is a brilliant mechanic and can make a bicycle sing.

It just so happened that I had this Sunday morning free, which was a very rare occurrence for me. Between work, family, church, and community obligations, I usually had almost no free time. But this weekend was an exception, so I accepted Scott's invitation and began writing down directions to his house. "Turn here, go four miles, turn left at dumpster, look for sign saying Monroe Institute, and go past it onto dirt road for one-half mile ..."

"What kind of institute?" I asked.

"Oh, they run conferences there, some government stuff," Scott said. "They are really nice people. They let us use their place for our wedding and would not take any money for it." And I did not think any more of it.

So, on the following crisp, fall Sunday morning, I found myself driving along unfamiliar country roads, enjoying the scenery and the rare peace of being away from the demands of work and family. I crested a hill and saw a beautiful panorama of the Blue Ridge Mountains off in the distance. The sun was bright, very clear, and the colors dazzled my eyes as I passed an unpretentious clump of wooden buildings on my left. The sign said, "Monroe Institute." The pavement stopped there, and I proceeded down a narrow dirt road to Scott's humble cabin, surrounded by roaming chickens and turkeys.

I could go on to describe many coincidences that occurred on that road over the next several years, but I will share just a few, one of which was my introduction to Robert Monroe. After visiting Scott on that beautiful fall Sunday, I began to wonder about the place I had passed at the top of the hill. I went to the local bookstore and bought all of Robert Monroe's books: *Journeys Out of the Body*, *Far Journeys*, and *Ultimate Journey*, and read them with interest—enough interest that I decided to talk with him. I opened the phone book and looked up "Monroe" and saw "The Monroe Institute of Applied Sciences." This was a title I liked, so I dialed the number, and when the receptionist answered, I asked to speak with Mr. Monroe.

"In reference to what?" she asked.

"I'm an anesthesiologist in town, and I want to ask Mr. Monroe some questions. Perhaps we could have lunch?"

"He's not in right now, but I'll give him your message."

The next day, I received a phone message inviting me to lunch. It turned out that I had said the magic word, "anesthesiologist." Robert Monroe—whom I came to know as Bob—was working on a study to help people undergoing anesthesia and surgery and was looking for anesthesiologists to help. A few days later, we met, and I found myself facing a frail, gray, elderly man smoking a cigarette—not my idea of what a modern-day mystic should look like. But Bob was friendly, and after a few minutes, I felt comfortable talking with him.

I told him about Brian's death, and he did not seem in the least bit surprised. "That was a pre-death cognition," he said with an almost bored tone. He was more interested in discussing the anesthesia and surgery project. So we talked about designing some studies—which was part of my job at the university. Though I did not learn much from Bob at this first meeting, it was clear that he had much to teach me.

Bob Monroe, I learned, had been a highly successful radio producer and entrepreneur who was experimenting with different sound patterns in the 1940s when he discovered that some of them gave him dreamlike out-of-body experiences. After many years of using these sounds for his own personal exploration of consciousness, he established his institute to help others on their own inner journeys.

The Monroe Institute (TMI) is a nonprofit center where people come together for weeklong meditation retreats aided by Bob's sound technology to help them experience altered states of consciousness. The institute does not advertise, and as a result, most people find their way there like I did—by coincidence. This is how Joe McMoneagle, the remote viewer, got there, along with many others including Dr. Elizabeth Kübler-Ross. In fact, many modern-day mystics have been there and were friends of Bob. (Bob died in 1995.)

Bob and his staff first taught me to meditate, and though it is a highly personal experience, I learned that a good teacher and a group pursuing the spiritual journey together are of enormous help. Much of the experience is similar to the dream state, except that you are awake and more easily remember what happens. There is a term called "lucid dreaming," described by Carlos Castaneda in *The Art of Dreaming*, wherein you know that you are dreaming and can consciously change the dream. Lucid dreaming is similar to the imagery of deep meditation, and both experiences are useful for the exploration of consciousness.

## A Waking Dream

My first meditation retreat at TMI, called "Gateway," was in the fall, a year and a half after Brian died. During this week, I had many new and unusual experiences and began to understand the language of consciousness. Needless to say, it was mind-expanding in many ways. On the last full day of the course, I noticed my grief for Brian growing strong, and I thought about Kathryn's recent dreams of him. She said Brian was changing, growing older, and did not seem to need us anymore. Kathryn seemed comforted by these dreams. I was envious and wanted my own contact with Brian. So, I decided to create a dream and invite him into it. I had heard that this was possible.

With this intention, at the beginning of the day's last meditation session, I entered a dream state, and focusing on my love for Brian, I created an imaginary garden. There, I placed many of the wonderful things Brian and I had shared together: a gentle waterfall we had once hiked to; beautiful flowers that created a wonderful aroma like the ones that grew around our house; bright iridescent hummingbirds flitting about, making their squeaking sounds; and soft, moist grass to walk on in bare feet like we used to do together. Then I created a little terrace surrounded by stones—a safe, comfortable place for a reunion.

Having finished my construction, I opened my heart and poured out all the love that I had known for this small, skinny boy whom I missed so immensely. I felt so much more love for him than I had known while he was alive. It reached down deeper than anything I had ever felt, right to the very roots of my being—into a richness and vastness I had never experienced before. It was this, the love I had never adequately expressed to him, which I placed into the garden within the border of the stones, and then I waited.

In a few moments, I felt a stirring in my heart, and a cloud began to take shape—condensing into Brian as I last remembered him. I rushed over and put my arms around him, feeling his bony, frail body. "Oh! Brian, I am so glad to see you!" I said, as I hugged him to me. But something felt wrong—something was missing. This was his body, but there was no emotion connecting us. Then I noticed that Brian was becoming hard and cold to my touch. I released him and, stepping back, saw that he was transforming into a stone statue. The energy that had been within his body drew into a ball of light behind the statue—beyond my reach. A sadness and understanding came over me as I said to him, "That's all right, Brian. I understand. I still love you even if you've changed and can't be what I want you to be." Then the ball of light moved away, traveling faster than anything I had ever seen, and disappeared.

As it vanished, I was left in the garden, brokenhearted. I felt completely empty, losing all desire to stay where I was. Softly, I found myself floating up and out of the garden into the blackness that surrounded it. As I entered the void, I felt a great tiredness overcome me. I had tried to reunite with Brian, but despite all my effort, I could not make it work. *If I can find someplace to rest, that would feel good,* I thought. Then, after a few moments, I noticed a huge object spinning slowly above me, illuminated by a pure and brilliant light. As I floated nearer, I could see that it was an enormous vortex made of stone, resembling a huge seashell.

*This looks like a good place to rest,* I thought. And so I settled within its coils, being warmed by the clear light shining into it. It felt good to finally rest. Most of my life I had worked hard to make things happen, and for the first time I could remember, I did not want to do anything—just rest and be carried along into nothingness.

As I became comfortable in the stillness, I felt a familiar presence on the stone next to my lap. It was a chipmunk—Brian's favorite animal. The little creature crawled into my lap, looked into my eyes, and as it did, I felt an enormous wave of love—Brian's love. I felt him so clearly, only now he was in the form of a small, lovable creature, who could love me as I loved him, for no other reason than because it was our nature. And so this enormous wave of love flowed between us as we spun together in space.

I had never experienced such emotion before—boundless and pure. Then, after a timeless moment, the dream was over, and I was returned to the awareness of my surroundings. My heart overflowed with love as my eyes overflowed with tears. My offering of love in the dream garden was multiplied manyfold, but it did not come as I had expected. The boundless love I received had not come through my memories of the past. It only came through my openness in the present, and when it did, I was grateful.

I thought about this dream over the following months and realized that my offering of love in the dream garden had been impure. Along with my unconditional love for Brian were mixed the clinging needs I had attached to him. These were the things that I had wanted from him that he could not give me. Of this, the Sufi poet, Rumi, writes, "Love is the flame that once kindled, burns everything, and only the mystery and the journey remain." In the flame of unconditional love, my neediness burned away, and only the mystery and my journey through it remained.

The grieving parents at The Compassionate Friends taught me that you must have the love of something before you can let it go. Brian's dream showed me that sometimes, when you let go—you get something more.

## Letting Go Every Day

My experiences at TMI were so powerful that I returned home in a daze, only to be greeted by a sick child and a frazzled wife—which quickly grounded me. I had been to my own personal mountaintop, felt my life changing direction, and my wife would not even let me talk about it. My head was spinning. What was I to do? As I pondered my dilemma over the next few months, I also began to notice that I was having an increasing number of mystical experiences in my daily life. I would be reading a book, for example, and see a typographical error on the page, but I would look again, and it would be gone. Then, when I turned to the next page, it would be there for real. I would watch Kathryn playing cards, feel a warmth in my heart, and "see" in her cards what she was going to draw next. I also noticed that when I talked with someone, I commonly had the thought of what they were going to say an instant before they said it. These experiences were unpredictable, though, and of little use, except to remind me that such things were possible.

Reality was becoming different for me now, and I could see that Brian's gifts had not died with him. Some lived on through me. But I did not know what to make of these new experiences. My life was no better or easier for all the mystical occurrences, and I still had the same nagging problems at home and work. Was there a way to use my new abilities to help manage my everyday problems? Was there some way to connect my mountaintop experience to my everyday life? I did not have a clue. But a fellow named Soon Young, a Qi Gong healer from Malaysia, did.

I met Soon Young at my first TMI Professional Division meeting, about six months after my Gateway retreat. He had been brought to the meeting by a Canadian psychology professor of Asian descent, who had been impressed with Soon Young's abilities. The professor asked him to give a talk and demonstrate his healing technique for the members: master's- and doctorate-level professionals from around the world—many first-rate minds with a foot in both the physical and nonphysical worlds. I looked forward to meeting these people, and I was not disappointed because a lot happened over the next six days.

There were daily scientific presentations of recent work, often using the Monroe sound technology (called Hemi-Sync®) to facilitate learning or healing of some sort. The most interesting events, however, were usually spontaneous. For example, a retired NASA engineer from Houston (one of the original Apollo flight directors) gave a two-evening workshop on shamanic journeying. The first evening resulted in the suggestions for my daughter, Lyn, which I have already described. Another journey that same night took me deep within the earth where I became caught in a molecular world and needed all of my willpower to break free. It was similar to a dream I had on that Christmas Eve in Hershey, Pennsylvania, when Kathryn had told me about her shared dream of Brian. I had been envious of her experience, gone back to sleep, and found myself in an underground world of glowing, tan-colored tunnels with forces trying to lure me deeper with promises of finding a missing child. I could feel their cold, emotionless intention to entrap me—the same feeling I had in the shamanic, molecular world.

Coincidentally, a few weeks before the TMI Professional Division meeting, I read an exact description of these glowing, tan tunnels in a Carlos Castaneda book. This is the domain of primitive forces that try to entrap and possess us, what Castaneda calls the "inorganic" or "elemental" world. The apostle Paul also describes these forces of possession in the Bible. How interesting to have the tunnel dream, then read about it, have a similar experience during the shamanic journey at TMI, read about it in the Bible, and then talk to others at the meeting who have had similar experiences. These were subjective, "inner" experiences, but they could be compared and validated to some degree.

The second day of the meeting, I met Soon Young. He gave his presentation to the group, answered questions, and then sat next to me at lunch. Soon Young was a pleasant, easygoing Asian man in his forties. He spoke fluent English, had a good sense of humor, and wore plain Western clothing. He explained that he had been an accountant but became interested in Qi Gong after many years of Kung Fu training. Soon Young said that he learned his healing technique from his own meditation, which he did for two to three hours each day. Another six to eight hours a day were spent in a busy healing practice at his home in Malaysia.

Qi Gong, Soon Young explained, uses the life force (chi) that Kung Fu warriors call upon to give them mystical powers. The height of Kung Fu mastery is to be able to disable an opponent from across the room without touching him. Qi Gong healers use this same force to heal and, "Would I like a demonstration?" he asked.

"Sure," I replied.

So we arranged to meet later that afternoon, and Soon Young told me I could bring others along, too. I invited two acquaintances I had met the day before: the director of special education for a school system and an MD-PhD medical researcher—both bright and talented men about my age. We met Soon Young in the exercise room, and he gave each of us a ten-minute healing session. He had us sit on a stool in the middle of the room and tell him what we wanted to heal. Then Soon Young moved around the person, assuming different poses while projecting energy out through his hands. Nothing much seemed to happen to the other two men, so I was not impressed.

When it was my turn, I hopped on the stool, and Soon Young asked me what I wanted to heal. After a few seconds of thought, I said that I wanted better posture. (All my life people have told me to "stop slouching.") Then Soon Young assumed his Qi Gong poses while moving around me. As he did this, I felt the urge to sit up straighter, which I consciously did. But I also began to feel very hot as my body continued to straighten, and I began to wonder who was controlling it. The heat continued to build up, and the sweat began to pour off of me, soaking through my shirt. When my session ended, we thanked Soon Young and left the room, the other men commenting on my sweaty condition. They both said that they had not felt anything special during or after the session. I began to cool off and, after saying good-bye to the others, went back to my room to shower and change clothes. Then I rejoined the meeting and did not think much more of it.

Later that night, though, something began to happen. I developed a tender spot over the end of my tailbone, the place that contacts the chair when I do not sit up straight. And by the next morning, it had become an open sore that forced me to sit up straight to get my weight off of it. Now, several years later, I can summarize my experience with this condition. Despite the best medical care, no physician has been able to make this sore go away. The only thing that works is to sit up straight. If I do that, the sore goes away, and if I slouch, it comes back. So, I guess the moral of this story is, be careful of what you wish for.

Returning to my time with Soon Young—I had some understanding of the chi force he was describing because, years earlier while an army officer, I had studied Tae Kwon Do with a sixth-degree black belt in Korea. He had taken us to a mountaintop monastery to train in the traditional "way," and I found the mental training to be especially interesting. It felt like unfinished business, and so, I wanted to learn more about Soon Young's abilities.

He agreed to give a four-day workshop in the evenings, and several of us studied with him. The principles were simple enough: you enter a meditative state, contact the healing energy within yourself, and project it out of your hands in certain poses. On the last day of the workshop, after we had learned the theory and techniques—all the mental information—Soon Young struck a pose and projected his healing power to each of us. It was similar to the feeling I had when Jackie shared her ability to find four-leaf clovers—a warm feeling of heart connection. Soon Young told us to meditate in the Qi Gong positions for one hour every day for three years, and then we could begin working as healers ourselves.

So I began a daily meditation practice that complemented my yearly meditation retreats. The retreats brought unpredictable, overwhelming experiences, and the daily practice helped me to integrate them into my life. I also found that my daily practice helped me to better manage recurring conflicts I was having. As I meditated on my loneliness after Brian's death, for example, I became aware of why I had clung to my memories of him so much: because I have trouble being close to other people, and that is because I am afraid. To be a friend is to be open and vulnerable, and I had not been willing to give up my lifelong defenses. I decided to change, and with that, feelings, thoughts, and dreams floated into my consciousness.

I felt the pain of my loneliness. *What could be worse than this?* I thought. *Next time you are with someone, see if you are willing to give up your loneliness—just a little bit, and see what happens.* A scene entered my mind. It was a party full of strangers, and I could feel my belly and chest tighten with fear. I observed it and felt its hold begin to relax. *It really doesn't matter what I say or do, or what the stranger says or does—does it?* I thought. *It only matters that my belly stays soft like I learned at Brian's funeral. Those were the best hugs—the soft bellies up against mine. If anyone wants to open to me, I will remember that feeling and try to answer—facing them with belly out—and see what happens.* And I found that it worked. I began to make friends more easily. I could see how others kept their bellies tight and guarded, and now I understand with compassion. This is how I know a problem is healed: when conflicts go away and I become more compassionate and understanding than before.

Since Brian's death, I have had many mystical experiences, and when the powerful, blow-me-away moments come, it is because I am feeling the same pure love that I felt with Brian in the center of the vortex. This is always what powers the big changes, and it is incredibly intelligent, arranging experiences with split-second timing in ways I could not have imagined. And when it is done with me, I see things in new ways.

One thing I have seen is that to heal, I need to feel two things: pure love and pure pain—thoughts are almost secondary. They are the changing faces covering the timeless, essential qualities I need to heal. At the center of every problem, often masked, is the pain of something that needs healing. If I can find this pain—focus on it—then feel the love from the vortex, something always comes together. I need not understand it all, just accept the thoughts, feelings, and experiences that come. Sometimes I heal parts of myself, and sometimes I heal into something larger, but the process always involves feelings of love and pain.

## A NEW LIFE

Two years after Brian's death, Kathryn and I celebrated the birth of a new son. Matthew (his name means "gift of God") was as beautiful a baby as I have seen, with blond hair and blue eyes—which was a surprise since Kathryn and I are both dark. (Kathryn has heard her share of "mailman" jokes.) Everything came so easily for him, and we delighted in our first healthy child. At last we had an easy baby, and by the time he was nine months old, everything at home was settling down into a pleasant routine. So, I felt free to take some time to attend my second TMI retreat, called "Guidelines," which was to bring me another life-changing moment.

It was a week of wonderful experiences that reminded me of the harmony I felt when Brian died. As the week went on, more and more coincidences began to occur until every chance meeting and casual remark became a gift. It was like pieces of a puzzle coming magically together. A meditation would create a powerful dream state that left me with many questions, which would then be answered by the events of the day. It got so that everything I observed became significant and meaningful. Finally, as all my experiences were acting in synchrony, I entered a state of meditation and experienced the timeless unity that was creating it all.

Upon my return to normal consciousness, I was surprised that the intense feelings I had were the same as when Brian died. When he died, the pain and sorrow were accompanied by a joy that I did not expect. Now I expected the joy, but not the pain and sorrow I was feeling. Buddhists call this the "ten thousand joys and ten thousand sorrows"— the paired feelings that come with personal transformation. Old ways of seeing and connecting with the world die as new connections and possibilities appear in a spiritual rebirth. I imagine this is the feeling of a butterfly first pushing out of its cocoon or a baby chick emerging from its egg. It is awakening to a larger, unknown world of possibility— awakening to a larger egg.

The chick can only hide and dream
until its shell is broken.
Then wings unfold and life unfolds
in symmetry unspoken.

# Chapter 5
# Stories of Loss and Healing

## A Tale of Two Deaths

Fred, our trusty old coonhound, was in decline, and I wondered what I should do for him. I never liked the idea of taking a dog to the vet, the place it feared most, and then sticking it with a needle to have it "put to sleep." Being an anesthesiologist, I never liked that choice of words either. Try telling a frightened five-year-old, about to have surgery, that you are going to "put them to sleep" and see what happens. "Like Fluffy?" they shriek, eyes big as saucers—bolting for the door. No, the idea that death and sleep are the same does not work for kids having surgery, and the idea of killing a beloved family member did not work for me either. *But that is what most people do,* I thought. *Maybe they know something I don't.*

Fred was a respected member of our family, and I wanted to protect him from fear in his final days. Fred deserved the best. He had been with our family from the time Brian was one and in the midst of his many surgeries. A week after we got Fred, we found out that Kathryn was pregnant with Lyn. So, given all we were going through, it was a blessing that Fred turned out to be such a great dog. Before we got him, Kathryn had researched the best family dogs and then cruised the SPCA, looking for puppies. When a litter of squirming coonhound pups showed up, Kathryn picked out Fred, and a few days later, I drove to the animal shelter to take him home.

Fred was cute, about eight weeks old, and jumping out of his skin with excitement as I put him in a box in the back of my car. As I drove out of the parking lot, I looked in the rearview mirror and saw his little head and front paws pop up over the rear seat. *I hope he stays in the back,* I thought, worried that he might get tangled up in my feet and cause an accident. But little Fred bravely struggled up and over the back seat and then made his way up to the front, wiggling up and over my armrest and then settling into my lap in a warm, loveable ball for the rest of the trip home. I never had to worry about anything with Fred.

Coonhounds are bred for their ability to track and kill raccoons, so they are big, smart, and tough animals. Dog show judges, I am told, allow coonhounds with battle scars from raccoon fights because it shows that they are good hunters. But they are also, surprisingly, one of the best dogs with children, and Fred was certainly remarkable in this and other ways. His first night at home, I put some newspaper down in his enclosure in the laundry room to paper-train him. I watched Fred, and when he peed on the floor, I said, "No," and put him on the paper. Fred understood what I wanted right away, and from then on, he did all his "numbers" on the paper. Flushed with success, the next day, I took away the newspaper, and when Fred looked like he wanted to pee, I took him outside. Then, when he peed on the grass, I praised him again, and that one time was all it took—he was housetrained and never had an accident after that.

Fred gave us a lot of love and support throughout all the trauma of Brian's medical procedures, and he kept the raccoons away from our garbage. But it was with our baby, Lyn, that Fred earned our greatest admiration. When Lyn was nine months old, her continual screaming from colic gave way to a continual, irritating whine that really grated on our nerves. Only later did we understand that this was because she was frustrated—she wanted to roll over, but her body would not respond.

Around her first birthday, Lyn was diagnosed with cerebral palsy, and the physical therapists gave us some exercises for her. Fred, being Lyn's devoted playmate, naturally helped with these. Although he was a frisky adolescent, Fred was always perfectly gentle with Lyn, and he nuzzled her and played with her on the floor until, eventually, she did roll over. And then, Lyn's irritating whine went away, and she became the sweetest child you can imagine.

Fred would let baby Lyn climb on top of him and pull his ears, always without complaint. Lyn's first word was "Fre(d)," and when Lyn made her first attempts to crawl, it was Fred she crawled to. So, you can see how he became an honored member of the family and Lyn's best friend. Fred was also a trusty companion for the rest of us, too. But now he was thirteen, hobbled by arthritis, and having trouble just getting around. *What would be the best thing to do for him?* I wondered. *Take him to the vet to be killed, or let him suffer?* I did not know, but I trusted that Fred, in some way, would help us know us what was best.

As we struggled with this dilemma, Kathryn was also faced with another unexpected problem when her good friend, Phyllis, was diagnosed with terminal ovarian cancer. Phyllis had moved to our town years before and contacted Kathryn (the only pastoral counselor in the area) to see if she could help Phyllis set up a spiritually centered counseling practice. The two of them hit it off right away and soon became great friends, going into practice together. Phyllis was divorced and—like us—had lost one of her children years earlier. She also had a mentally handicapped daughter about Lyn's age, and since they shared many of the same special activities, we ended up spending a lot of time together.

Phyllis was also a godsend for me because, although I could talk about spiritual matters with my friends at TMI, I could not talk about such things at home. Kathryn, being a pastoral counselor, considered the spiritual world as her domain and did not want me messing about in it. Phyllis, on the other hand, could talk about her spiritual experiences with Kathryn and often did. Phyllis had been attending another spiritual center in our area for many years, and after hearing about it, Kathryn became curious and started going there with Phyllis. After a while, all the things that Kathryn would not talk to me about, she would talk about with Phyllis—for hours. They spent many happy weekends together at the spiritual center over several years—engaging in activities like sweat lodges, discussions groups, and puppy piles. As a result—thanks again to Phyllis—I could now talk about my spiritual adventures with Kathryn.

Now that Phyllis had become such a close friend, the thought of losing her was troubling Kathryn. So, with the impending loss of both

Phyllis and Fred on our minds, I came home after work one day to find a surprise. I got out of my car and started walking to the house when I looked up to find a mass of about sixty vultures roosting in a tree on the south side of our house. I had never seen anything like it. What was going on? I wondered. *Oh yes!* I realized. *Phyllis and her daughter are coming for dinner tonight. I guess the vultures know that Phyllis is going to die soon.*

I showed the vultures to my family, and an hour later, Phyllis and her sixteen-year-old daughter, Pam, arrived. We visited, ate dinner, made small talk, and after a few hours, we said good-bye. Phyllis was in denial about her cancer, so the conversation was awkward—especially since I am sure that Pam knew something was wrong. Kathryn and I wanted to respect Phyllis's wishes, but we were also trying to take care of Pam—and doing both was not easy.

With this conflict bubbling at the back of my mind, the next morning, I went outside and noticed that about half of the vultures had gone from our tree. Still, thirty black, ominous birds hanging over your house is an impressive sight. *What is going on now?* I wondered—and then it came to me. *I'll bet the vultures are telling us that Fred is going to die soon, too—and I'll bet he will show us how to do it.* And that is what happened. So, over the next two months, I was given a lesson in how differently two beings can die.

Phyllis, aided by some overly optimistic comments from her doctors, steadfastly refused to admit that she was dying and, therefore, refused to plan anything. Even though her daughter, Pam, could clearly see that something was seriously wrong, we could not discuss it and we could not make plans for Pam's future. This charade became even harder to manage as Phyllis's cancer spread, and she got sicker. To their credit, Phyllis's spiritual community gathered around her and gave her the best around-the-clock care. After several weeks of this, though, the helpers were becoming worn down from all the work. Mercifully, Phyllis slipped into a coma and was taken to the hospital, which gave all the caregivers a breather. This would have been an easy way to go—slip into a peaceful sleep and quietly stop breathing a few days later.

But Phyllis had told her doctors to do everything they could for her, so they plugged her into an IV, corrected the chemistry imbalance that had caused her coma, and when Phyllis woke up, they sent her home again. If Phyllis had made some use of this extra time, I might have understood the wisdom of it all, but she did not—at least, not that anyone could tell. Phyllis stayed in denial even though her body was breaking down, and it all started to feel a little crazy. The caregivers went back to their grueling shifts, juggling their own lives and trying to get some sleep, while trying to keep Phyllis as comfortable as they could. But this was getting increasingly difficult as Phyllis was getting more miserable and needing a lot more care.

Fred, on the other hand, was declining gracefully. He spent his time on the bed we made for him in the sunroom, with food and water within easy reach. Fred quit moving around after a while, and then he stopped eating. Once a day, though, he would struggle to his feet and go outside for a few minutes, sometimes getting confused. So we would turn him around and point him in the right direction, and he would look in our eyes and a glimmer of recognition would appear. "Oh, yes, I know and trust this person," he seemed to be saying. This jogged his memory enough to get him to walk back inside again. After two weeks of this, Fred quit drinking and did not get up again—sleeping most of the time.

A few days later, I was at work when Kathryn called me. "I think Fred is dying," she said, "is there anything I should do?" I told her to get *The Tibetan Book of Living and Dying* from my bookshelf and see if there was anything it suggested. Unlike Western culture, the Tibetan Buddhists do not shy away from death. To the contrary, the moment of death is extremely important to them, and many prepare for it all their lives. This preoccupation even gets a little ridiculous sometimes with Buddhist priests trying to out do each other in how they master their final moments.

Sometimes a priest will send out invitations saying he is going to leave his body at a certain day and time so everyone can come and participate. There are tales of a monk who invited people to watch him die while he performed a headstand. Not to be outdone, another monk in attendance stood up and announced that he would die while walking—keeling over in mid-stride. So, you can see that Tibetans are not shy about death at all. If anything, they revel in it. And if you believe in reincarnation like they do, death (or anything else for that matter) is not such a big deal. After all, who cares when it happens, when you can have as many lives and as much time as you want?

So Fred, you could say, was more Buddhist in his dying than
Phyllis—no big deal—making it easier to take care of him, the closer
he got. Finally, when the children were at school, Fred quietly slipped
into a coma, and Kathryn noticed that his breathing had changed. It
was then that she called me, got the book, and read it with Fred's head
resting in her lap. Kathryn said that Fred went through all the stages,
just like the book described, and when he finally stopped breathing,
he just was not there anymore—not in that old, worn-out body. He
did not seem to suffer. Though Kathryn had been trained as a minister
and hospital chaplain, Fred was the first being she had actually watched
die.

I left work early so I could be home before the children arrived
from school. It was a beautiful fall day, and we chose a grave site on a
hill overlooking the meadow that had been Fred's domain—with the
colorful mountains in the distance catching the last of the sun's rays.
The children came home, and we told them that Fred had died. (They
had been expecting it.) We had a funeral service, and each of us had
a chance to express our gratitude for the time and love that Fred had
shared with us. We told him that we would always remember him, and
then we petted him one last time. But he was not there to the touch,
and so we buried his old, worn-out body. Fred always took good care of
us, and now he showed us that that we could love and care for him all
the way through to the end, and everything was okay. I never needed
to worry about anything with Fred.

Around the time that Fred died, Phyllis returned home from the
hospital after her coma. She hung on to life for another difficult month
and finally slipped into her final coma. She returned to the hospital
where she was put in a room by herself and died a short while later.
When the spiritual community heard that Phyllis had finally expired,
everyone was so exhausted that they breathed a collective sigh of relief.
Not only could they begin to rest, but finally, they were released from
Phyllis's denial. Her family and friends could now begin to talk about
their feelings, plan for the future, and grieve her loss.

The spiritual community processed what had happened and learned
from their experience. Kathryn and I, though, had the best lesson
because Fred was such a good teacher. Both he and Phyllis suffered
as their bodies began to fail. But Fred, living in the moment, suffered
less as his death drew near. Phyllis, in contrast, fought her death and

suffered all the more for it—right up to the end. When all was done, though, both beings found their natural peace.

## STAGE MOTHER

I love going to the theater so whenever Kathryn and I go out for the evening, a play is usually my first choice for entertainment. One summer, the local theater company, Live Arts, performed a black comedy, *Sister Mary Explains It All*, to a sold-out audience as part of its Summer Theater Festival. Kathryn and I went to the opening and enjoyed the play immensely, laughing uproariously with the crowd and delighting in the play's social commentary. So the following spring, when I got a flyer in the mail calling for directors for the upcoming summer theater season, I had the bright idea to try directing a play myself. I had not acted since high school and never directed anything, so this was not a rational decision by any means.

The next week, I went to the aspiring directors' meeting and selected a play (another black comedy) from the pool of possibilities. The following week, I pitched it to the company's artistic director, and a few days later, he notified me that my play was selected as one of the eight productions for the festival. We were also given the main stage, where *Sister Mary* had been performed. My family and I discussed the extra time I would have to devote to the project (I estimated ten to twenty hours per week, but it turned out to be twice that), and they gave me permission to go ahead. So, with visions of sold-out crowds laughing hysterically at my play, I committed to the three-month-long project. The whirlwind of activity started immediately with the casting auditions, and to prepare, I stopped off at the local bookstore and library and got all the books on directing I could find. A week later, after I had studied the books and planned and cast the play, I got a phone call.

I was at home one evening, washing the dishes, when the phone rang. I could see from the caller ID that it was my mother, which usually meant trouble. I cautiously picked up the phone, said hello, and heard my mother's unusually soft voice.

"Gregg, I'm dying," she whispered and then coughed.

"What?" I replied, astonished. "What happened?"

"I've got lung cancer, and I told the doctors I didn't want any treatment. I need you to come up, right away," she said with finality.

In shock, I scrambled to find my schedule. "Okay, wait a minute … I can come up next week," I said.

"No, I need you up here now!" she replied then gasped and went into a coughing fit.

*Oh my God!* I thought. *She must be in worse shape than I imagined.* So, I frantically poured over my work schedule again and said, "Okay, I'm on call tomorrow night, that's Thursday, so I'm off on Friday. If I can get a good flight, I can be there by Friday afternoon."

"Good, I'll see you then," she whispered, coughed, and then hung up.

"Kathryn!" I called out. "My mother's dying, and I have to go to Chicago on Friday!"

"What?" she asked.

I explained what little I knew, called to make arrangements at work and with the play, and made travel reservations. I slept fitfully, and then, early the next morning, I went to work with my suitcase already packed.

I worked all day in the operating room and then well into the night, taking care of the emergency cases that make up the usual night fare. Then at 5:30 AM, I tanked up on coffee and left the hospital, driving the one and a half hours to Richmond to catch my flight. Usually, I try to take it easy after being on call because I have discovered that as I get older, I am much more impaired than in my younger years. Just one or two phone calls in the middle of the night, and the next morning, I would miss an exit while driving, make stupid mistakes, and need a nap.

But, obviously, this was a stretch that I was going to have to make. So, buzzing on caffeine and adrenaline, I drove into the sunrise to make my flight to Chicago. The connections went well, and my flight landed on time. I called my mother from the airport and told her I would arrive as planned. Then I took the shuttle to the hotel near Mom's apartment, checked in, and walked the two blocks to her apartment building in a fashionable part of town.

The last time I had seen my mother, a few months earlier, she was her usual flamboyant self: hiding her age well, wheeling and dealing with friends in tow, frequenting stylish restaurants—and always avoiding the check at all costs. Mom had changed her name after her last divorce to sound more glamorous and fancied herself as Auntie Mame (from the popular play of that name)—breaking through everyone's humdrum existence, failing gloriously at everything she tried—yet always redeemed by her heart of gold. At least, that is how she saw herself. And maybe there were times in my childhood when I curled up in her lap, enveloped by the motherly love that flowed from this heart of gold, but I cannot remember any. Instead, I just recall a parade of new boyfriends, new apartments, and new schools. Isolated and rootless, we drifted around the apartment buildings and frigid streets of Chicago, as I tried to learn my way around the new neighborhoods.

When I was ten, Mom remarried my father, and we moved four times in five years before she divorced him again. During this time, we had two dogs at different times, but they both went crazy, and we had to get rid of them. By the time Mom and Dad divorced for the second time, my father had become rich from the family business he had inherited, and Mom got a lot of money from the settlement. But between her expensive lifestyle and falling prey to investment sharks who got their hands on her money by flirting with her, she quickly became broke. "No regrets," she would say. "I was always a player."

In her youth, Mom had been quite a beauty as well as a gifted artist. She had fashioned a career as an interior designer, but although talented, she could not deal with the organizational and people-skills part of the business—so it failed. Her dark beauty eventually faded, and her money disappeared. Unable to hold on to the simplest job and with only minimal Social Security benefits (since she had never paid into it), Mom became dependent on her rich sister, Judy, and me for money. Judy, the middle of the three sisters (Mom being the oldest) had always been the rock of the family and indulged Mom's whims much more than I could. Because of this, there was always tension between Mom and me. She constantly demanded more money and attention than I could give her.

These were the thoughts that flooded my mind as I approached Mom's apartment building, getting blasted by the wind off the nearby lakefront. The doorman let me in, and I took the elevator to her floor, smelling her perfume as I approached her door. I knocked and heard Mom answer, "Come in. It's open." I entered the apartment, greeted by an even stronger perfume smell, and walked into her bedroom. There I saw my diminutive mother sitting in bed in her gold pajamas, her face more thin and angular than before—but with good color, thanks to a skillful layer of makeup. Her hair was dyed dark brown and tied up in a knot; her dark brown eyes were not sad, and she did not look deathly ill. I leaned over and gave her a kiss on the cheek.

"How was your flight?" she asked.

"Good," I answered. "It was an easy connection and call wasn't too bad last night. I got some sleep."

We visited for a while, and she told me the details of her medical condition. Two years earlier, she had been diagnosed with a rare but easily curable form of breast cancer—but she refused any treatment. Then, a week ago, while visiting Judy at her ranch in Colorado, Mom developed a worsening cough. The local doctor got a chest x-ray that showed cancer throughout her lungs. Whether it was from the breast cancer or her lifelong smoking was not known, and since Mom did not want any treatment, there was no point in doing a biopsy to find out. The doctor sent Mom back to Chicago where her regular doctor told her that she was terminal and arranged for hospice care.

As she was finishing the story, there came a knock at the door. I opened it to find a pleasant, professional-looking woman in her thirties carrying a medical bag. She was the hospice nurse, and when she explained the plan for Mom's care, I was most impressed by her compassion and competence. She left after an hour—followed by a parade of friends, nurses, and therapists throughout the afternoon. And through it all, Mom remained the center of attention: weak, coughing, and in charge.

The plan for the evening, one of Mom's friends informed me, was dinner at her favorite restaurant. Since her birthday was two months away and no one thought she would live that long, tonight would be an early birthday party with all of Mom's best friends in attendance. The only question was, was Mom strong enough to do it? We all decided that we would try it and see. I was sent back to my hotel room to change clothes while Mom's friends—all successful, elderly women—got her ready for the party.

When I returned to the apartment at 6:00 PM, I was surprised at how much better Mom looked. She and her friends were dressed in their big-city finest, with sparkling jewelry and fashion accessories galore. All this dressing up seemed therapeutic too, since Mom was acting stronger and coughing less. We took her arms and walked her down to the elevator and out the door to a waiting cab. A few minutes later, we arrived at the hotel restaurant where Mom's other friends were waiting for us. We were now a party of seven—four fashionable women in their seventies and eighties, one elderly gay interior designer, Mom, and me.

The hostess took us to our table, and I noticed that we were the first people to be seated. As a result, our service was great, with waiters sliding all the ladies' chairs forward at the same time as they sat down and every plate of every delicious course hitting the table at the same moment. Water glasses were invisibly filled whenever heads were turned, and for a few hours, we wanted for nothing.

Mom rose to the festive occasion, stopped coughing altogether, and seemed to regain her strength, becoming the life of the party— laughing and joking with everyone, including the waiters. The old party girl in her was coming back to life—so much so that four hours later, as everyone else was fading, Mom was ordering another round of Grand Marnier and pumping up the conversation. Her laughter rang through the now-empty restaurant as the tired waiters looked on, obviously wanting us to leave so they could finish their work and go home.

What a difference a change of scene makes. Just five hours earlier at her apartment, Mom had been the dying princess, surrounded by grieving caregivers, waiting on her hand and foot. But now, in the restaurant, she was the vibrant hostess—still going strong as her audience—we of the exhausted, numb butts—were stifling our yawns, yet unable to tactfully tell this dying woman that we wanted her party to end. Mercifully, the waiter brought the check, and I put up an acceptable fight to pay it, gracefully losing out to the gay decorator. We got Mom back into a cab, took her home, and I returned to my hotel room and collapsed into bed—my forty-hour day finally coming to an end.

The next morning, I returned to Mom's bedside, but her deathbed act—now completely blown by last night's party scene—was gone, and so was most of her cough. Now that Mom was being more honest, we actually had a nice visit, going over old photo albums and then having lunch. After this, her friends, recovering from our marathon "last supper," began showing up again. It was now obvious to all of us that Mom was going to be around for a while and we needed to make some long-range plans. We put our heads together, found a good person to stay with her, and then I coordinated all the medical care with the hospice nurse. After lunch the next day, Sunday, I said good-bye and headed back home, trying to process all that had happened. On the way to the airport, I noticed that my face began to feel numb, almost like a mask, and the next day, I developed a strange rash on the front of my left thigh.

## Farewell Performance

To say that the next two months were hectic would not do it justice—dangerously out of control would be more accurate. My budding theatrical career was increasingly becoming a disaster before my eyes. On the positive side, I liked the play and was lucky enough to have cast some good actors. I was, also, extremely fortunate to have the local "grand dame" of the theater, Carol (a former Broadway actress and director), take me under her wing and tutor me throughout the whole production. Carol had studied with the greatest directors in the country and was an excellent teacher in her own right. So, I learned a lot about the life of the theater, and Carol told me that I had talent.

At the same time, however, the forces of theater evil were also raising their heads. First, I had cast a problem actor in the lead role, and though talented, he would not cooperate with me or the other actors. Of directing, it is said that 90 percent of success is determined by the casting, and I agree—it always comes down to the people. So, my lead actor had a personality problem, and he had recommended a friend of his to be the stage manager, the director's right-hand helper, who also turned out to be a problem. As Carol observed: "A stage manager is supposed to help the director, but this one is a thorn in your side."

Besides the cast problems, I discovered that I also had a play problem. The final production of the theater company's regular season was an offbeat musical, and when I went to see it, I turned to my wife and said, "Oh my gosh!" It was an almost exact copy of my play—a boy raised by animals (in my play, raccoons), who is then adopted by a demented veterinarian, then attacked by society. You are never supposed to produce two plays this similar in the same town, much less within weeks of each other. "The critics are going to harpoon me," I said—and they did.

Decades earlier, while a teenager, I had experienced a theatrical disaster at a summer camp where I was working. Being one of the few interested males, I had gotten a lead role in *South Pacific* and was doing well until one scene when a lifeboat unexpectedly appeared in the wings, blocking my entrance to the stage. Try as I might, I could not find a way to get onstage and so, the other actors had to improvise one of my important scenes without me. Then, in the next scene, I was supposed to sing "Younger than Springtime" to my beautiful costar, but shaken by the previous scene's problem, I created another one. My adrenalin was flowing so much—I kept speeding up my song so that I actually finished ahead of the piano (and the piano player was valiantly trying to keep up with me). My friends told me afterward that in all sincerity, it was probably the worst single performance in the camp's entire history. So I knew about theatrical disasters, and my current play looked like it was trying to turn into another one.

However, there is always hope, especially in the theater. So, after huge amounts of time and effort on the play, on top of a busy job and home schedule, on top of trips to Chicago every few weeks, by the morning of the play's opening, I was totally stressed out. As I drove to work, I saw a dead raccoon in the middle of the road. *Not a good sign,* I thought. After work, I got to my car only to find that the rear tire was completely flat and so was the spare. *Another bad sign,* I thought. A few hours later, I arrived at the theater and went backstage to give the actors their director's gifts and hand the play over to the stage manager for its run.

I went out into the almost empty theater to sit with Carol and my family and watched the play unfold. The few people who showed up (typical for the Summer Festival, I discovered—last year's sellout for *Sister Mary* had been an anomaly) laughed at the jokes, and the staging went well. But playing to an empty house felt empty. Musicians, I am told, do not need an audience as much as actors do, and I think this is because actors have more emptiness. The Russian director Stanislavski was the first to explain this. He realized that every action on the stage comes from a character trying to fill its emptiness. An actor's motivation, therefore, is always what the character is missing. So, whenever an actor gets stuck trying to bring his character to life, the director is supposed to ask him what the character wants at that moment and what the clearest action to show it is.

Every action on the stage occurs because every character *wants* something. And the actors want something, too—they want to feel their connection with the audience. Then the audience comes to see the play because they, also, want something—they want to feel their connection with the play. So, the characters, actors, and audience all gather in the theater, pooling their emptiness and hoping that something magical will come from it. And if the play is good, the audience relaxes, quits thinking (usually around the third act), and joins its magical world. You can feel it in the air when this happens, and when the play is over, the actors take this special feeling home with them, and the audience leaves enriched by a new experience.

But when the audience does not come, you can feel the difference because the drama loses its power to transform. The actors are left with an unshared story, and this is what I felt as I watched the play unfold. I had worked long and hard to provide the correct lighting, music, acting, and staging. But without an audience to connect with, the magic just did not happen. So, the play ran for two weeks, and the critics were outraged that it was an obvious steal of the previous production. The crowds stayed small, the actors lost their enthusiasm, and when it was finally over, I was relieved. Then, after the last performance, I flew back to Chicago to see my mother, for what would be the last time.

When I saw Mom this time, she really did look like she was dying. The melodrama was gone, and everything was now all too real; she really was weak, her cough was terrible, and she needed oxygen to help her breathe. Besides her declining health, Mom's support system had also been in decline. During the months of my drama project, I had watched as my mother created her own drama in her own life. Every week or two, she would fire her help, argue with the hospice nurse, and yell at her friends so that some of them stopped coming. Mom had always been selfish and manipulative, but she had usually done it with such style that she got away with it. But now her style was gone—the glamour and pretensions were gone—and she was driving people away. The friends who continued to come earned my admiration. I had to be there, but they did not.

"Why," I asked Mom's friends, "are you so loyal, even when she treats you all so badly?"

To this, all the successful, capable women pretty much gave the same answer: "Your mother was always so entertaining to be around, so unpredictable. She had an excitement for life that was worth all the selfishness. I liked being around her, and now it is my time to give her what I can." What they could give her was their competence—

something Mom had always been lacking. Remarkably inept in practical matters, she even had trouble changing a lightbulb. These women could do that and more, but they appreciated something in Mom that until now, I had not. They valued her spontaneity and artistic ability. This was what Mom had been giving to them.

We regrouped our forces, and over the next few days, the hospice nurse, remaining friends, and I cobbled together another care plan and hired another home health aide. On the final day of my visit, Mom told the hospice nurse that she had dreamt that her dead relatives were waiting for her, and the hospice nurse said this was a sign that Mom's death would be coming soon. Her birthday was August 12, a few days away, and her two sisters, Carole and Judy, were coming into town to spend it with her. Mom gave me some of her jewelry for Lyn and Matthew, and as I was helping her out of bed, I noticed that she had a rash on the front of her left thigh, identical to mine. "What is this from?" I asked, pointing to the red mark. "No one knows," she replied, "but it started when I got my cancer." Puzzled, I changed the subject.

We talked for another hour, and then I kissed Mom good-bye, told her that I loved her, and then I left for the airport. A few days later, I called Mom on her birthday, but she sounded weak and could not talk for long. Two days after that, as I was visiting my in-laws at the beach with my family, I got a call from my aunt Judy telling me that Mom had died in her sleep that morning. Judy said Mom wanted to be cremated without a service, so there was no point in my coming to Chicago. "We'll just have a headstone dedication in a few months," Judy said. I thanked her for all her help and hung up the phone.

*Nothing to do, just a phone call and your mother is dead,* I thought. *Seems like I should do something. Well, at least the suffering is over, and Mom can't cause any more trouble ... or so I thought.*

It is easy to remember the date and time of Mom's death because a few hours later, we heard the news of a rolling blackout—the biggest power failure in North American history, starting in the Midwest, then extending into Canada and down the East Coast. Amazingly, it stopped only a few miles from our house at the New Jersey Shore, not crossing the water of Barnegat Bay to affect us. The cause, we were told, was a tree branch that fell across a power line, causing a chain reaction the likes of which had never before been seen. Mom, I am sure, would be pleased to be going out with such a "bang." She always liked stirring things up and did so at every opportunity.

## Restless Spirit

As long as there have been humans, there have been mysteries. And the people who deal with them are often called mystics—although many modern religions now ignore their mystical roots. One of a mystic's common functions is to rid us of troublesome spirits because it is a common experience that people who cause trouble when they are alive, also cause trouble after they are dead. And that is what happened to me and to my aunt Judy. We had both taken care of Mom, Judy more than I, and Mom had latched on to both of us when she was alive. And now that she was dead, bad things happened for Judy, even more than for me.

Judy was Mom's younger sister and the most capable member of her family. She had married well and was now a widow in excellent health with a large and thriving family. But after Mom's death, Judy came down with an autoimmune disease—her body's immune cells attacking her own tissues. Judy lost the ability to walk, then to eat, and had to be fed through a tube in her nose. Four debilitating years later and weighing only eighty-five pounds, she finally died. This healthy, vibrant woman's life had taken a radical turn after Mom's death, and so did mine.

Before the difficult summer that ended with my mother's death, I had been a healthy fifty-six-year-old triathlon finisher, slow but steady, and with no medical problems. In the months after Mom's death, though, my masklike facial numbness got worse, and I developed a nervous tic in my left eye. A few months later, my wife noticed that the left side of my face suddenly drooped into a half-faced frown. I went to the emergency room where I was worked up for a possible stroke. The diagnosis, thankfully, turned out to be Lyme disease, and I responded to antibiotics, although some of the nerve damage was permanent.

Around this time, I also began to have chest and abdominal pain, high blood pressure, extremely painful upper leg cramps that would seize up in the middle of the night, and I became weak and irritable. My liver, the organ that removes toxins from the body, also began to show damage. In addition, I developed a constant tickle in the right side of my throat that made it difficult for me to talk since I would have to continually clear my throat or cough. My healthy life was gone, and I had become a debilitated, coughing, pill-popping mess—making frequent visits to my many doctors.

Meanwhile, my body's inner turmoil was matched by my life's outer problems. My work at the hospital was beset with political and safety problems, the likes of which I had never seen before. My anesthesia group was in such turmoil that, what had at one time been an ideal job, was now turning into a nightmare. It got so bad that I could not give my patients good care, and I was stymied in every attempt to fix the problems—not good for a perfectionist like me. Lawsuits were swirling around me (fortunately, I was not named in one), and after two years, it got so bad that I asked my wife what she thought about my quitting my job. We were at the New Jersey Shore on our last day of vacation, standing in the ocean waves when I asked her. I think we both realized that the stress from my work would probably kill me if I stayed there.

Keep in mind that we have a special needs child and that my entire net worth was about the same amount of money needed to take care of Lyn for the rest of her life. My income was important, and there were no other jobs in the area that I wanted. Also, we loved our home and community and had no desire to move, especially as I neared retirement age. So, we could not see a good solution to our problem. To Kathryn's credit, she said everything would be all right if I quit. It was going to be a leap of faith for both of us, and as it turned out, a fruitful one in ways we could not have imagined.

We drove home from the beach, and the very next day, the phone rang. My friend Chris (from race-car driving school) was calling to tell me that a new surgical center was being built in town and the owner needed an anesthesiologist who specialized in pain management. I called the owner, and by the following week, I had a new job. It was completely unexpected, unprecedented, and seemingly perfect—no nights or weekends, no sick patients, no politics, and I could have everything just the way I wanted. Also, since new surgical centers take a few years to get busy, I had another bonus, something I had not enjoyed since my college days: free time to spend with my family, get into shape, and to finish a writing project that had gotten stuck and abandoned—this book (the one thing my mother was interested in). What were the chances?

A week later, my doctor discovered that I had a benign tumor of my parathyroid gland that was causing my medical problems. I had the surgery to remove the tumor, and the surgeon found that it was wrapped around the nerve that goes to the right side of my throat. This was causing the tickle and cough that no physician could diagnose. So in less than an hour, my medical problems were cured, and all this happened within a few weeks of quitting my job and trusting my future to fate. A sick job and a sick body, cured in only weeks—what were the chances?

What would have happened if I had stayed in my old job and old life? I wonder. How long could I have withstood the pounding of my own misfortune? Would it have destroyed me like my aunt Judy? I am thankful that I will never know for sure. But there is a play about someone who struggles in a world where everything seems to be going badly. Shakespeare's Hamlet is a reasonable man in a "sea of troubles." His despair becomes so great that he considers suicide: "To be, or not to be"—to be pounded on by "outrageous fortune," or not to be alive at all. Hamlet does not see a good solution—and so, he is destroyed by the loveless world that, tragically, he cannot change.

I can understand how Hamlet felt because, in the midst of all my problems, I too could not change any of them by being reasonable. I acted reasonably at work, but the problems only got worse. I acted reasonably to calm my mother's restless spirit—meditating and asking for help from friends skilled in the mystical arts. I tried to understand what the grieving process wanted from me, but despite all this, nothing much changed. Only when I allowed my life to take a new and unplanned direction did my problems get better. What I did not realize at the time was that, to tame the restless spirit that was haunting my life, I had to claim its power as my own. I could not make my mother go away—I could only accept her dark offering. This was where fate was leading me, and if I had resisted and remained stuck in my old life—becoming humdrum, I think my mother would have killed me.

## ADVENTURES IN OZ

When I was in medical school, we had a presentation by Elizabeth Kübler-Ross, MD, who was famous for her work on death and dying. Her lectures were packed, and everyone acknowledged that she had made a great breakthrough in describing the stages of grief: denial, anger, depression, bargaining, and acceptance. At the time, I had no direct experience of grief, so I dutifully wrote down what she said and waited for the opportunity to use this new knowledge. But in my thirty years of medical practice, it never proved useful.

And later, when I lived through the deaths of Brian, Mom, Fred, Phyllis, and others, few of them or the people who grieved their loss went through any of these stages. Brian was the only one who changed much, going from depression to acceptance in his last few weeks. Phyllis stayed in denial to the end. Fred just got quiet. Mom stayed her usual, chaotic self with her usual flashes of anger—but no denial, bargaining, or depression. The only common stages of grief that I could see were shock and pain, lasting a few weeks, and then back to reality—dealing with the usual challenges of life, now with some new ones added on. We all pretty much stayed the same. Yet, something was clearly trying to happen—but what?

As I was pondering these weighty questions at home one day, I decided to watch a movie while exercising on my indoor bike trainer. I was looking for a documentary, but the only DVD I could find was *The Wizard of Oz*, so I popped it into my trusty iMac computer and was working up a good sweat by the time Dorothy makes it to the Land of Oz. After Dorothy assembles her entourage of characters—Tin Man, Scarecrow, Cowardly Lion, and Wicked Witch—it finally dawned on me why this is such a classic story—because the author, L. Frank Baum, is describing something that we all deal with everyday—loss. *The Wizard of Oz* is all about how we deal with the loss of something we love.

Dorothy is an orphan living with a family that has little time for her. To make matters worse, she is threatened with the killing of her dog, Toto—her main source of love and affection. As Dorothy is overwhelmed by this impending loss, she is carried off to the magical Land of Oz, where her cast of supporting characters assembles around her. The Tin Man (brains without heart), Scarecrow (heart without brains), Cowardly Lion (inner conflict), and the Wicked Witch (outer conflict) are all acting out the different ways that Dorothy can use to solve her problem.

You can also see how this works by watching a football game. There are the coaches (brains); the cheerleaders, band, and dancers—the artists who provide the spirit (heart); the players who pit themselves against the other team's players (outer conflict); and the trainers and managers who deal with the team's internal problems (inner conflict). Every group, when challenged, will split itself up into these fundamental roles to solve a problem, and when they are finished, they come back together again to celebrate and learn from their experience.

But if the challenge is too difficult to solve, the parts become frustrated and go to extremes. So, if a football team is struggling, the coach may argue with the officials, "Come on, Ref, give us a break!" (bargaining), the players may lose their tempers (anger), and people on the sidelines may become sad and tearful (depression). And yes, everyone goes to extremes at some time, but rarely do we get stuck there. If we do, though, we may get sent to a psychiatrist—like Dr. Kübler-Ross. So, when she described her stages of grief, she was really describing people so dysfunctional that they were referred to her for psychiatric care. Those were the kinds of cases she saw. And they are not so much "stages" of grief (that everyone goes through step-by-step) as they are "roles" of challenge, stuck in the dysfunctional extreme.

However, even in the extreme, there is something missing from the Kübler-Ross model. She identifies the dysfunctional behaviors of the Witch (anger), the Lion (depression), and the Tin Man (bargaining, intellectualizing, emotional detachment), but she leaves out the Scarecrow. Being a creature of feelings without thoughts, when stressed, the Scarecrow will become flighty and overly emotional. And the extreme forms of these irrational, negative feelings are anxiety and panic, which are as common as the other extreme behaviors.

So L. Frank Baum's story more completely describes how people deal with difficult challenges. And, true to form, the artist, Baum, had the vision decades before the scientist, Kübler-Ross, described it in technical terms. But besides describing our extreme behaviors, Baum also describes the normal behaviors we use in everyday problem solving—using our strongest qualities to tackle the easiest parts of the problems. Baum shows us how we use our strengths, and—brilliant storyteller that he is—he also shows us how we use our weaknesses. Like the director, Stanislavski, Baum understands that to make a good story, every character needs to have a weakness. The motivation for every character's action is always that they are missing something important from their life and need to find it.

One of my hobbies is leading groups of people through outdoor challenge courses at the University of Virginia. Sometimes the challenge is to get everyone up over a high wall or to find a path through a maze, and to make the problem more fun and meaningful, I always tell a colorful story to frame the activity. If I am working with students from the business school, for example, I might start by saying something like, "On the other side of this wall is your perfect first job with a great salary and a new car. Now all you have to do is get everyone over the wall and the job is yours." Every challenge begins with a story about how the group is missing something important and what they need to do to get it.

If I make the challenge too easy, though, the group will get bored. And, if I make it too difficult, the group will usually get frustrated and go to pieces—with the pieces becoming: mad, sad, detached, and anxious—all different ways of expressing the group's pain. A little experience of this can be useful because it shows the group that the challenge is too much for them, and teaches them when they need to ask for help.

Most of the time, though, I try to give the group a challenge that makes it split up into functional parts without going to extremes. This is when the group works the best, learns the most, and has the most fun. And when I watch groups split up, they always take on the same parts as the characters in the *Wizard of Oz*, and the parts always come in pairs. The individuals take on their preferred roles, and then they go looking for their missing partners. Someone becoming a bully (witch) will find a coward (lion), and someone becoming a tin man will find a scarecrow. They look for their missing quality, trying to be whole again.

### My Life as a Coward

When I was growing up, I was both a coward and a tin man, and I will tell you about being a coward first.

Always the new kid in school with no family or friends to back me up, I was skinny, weak, and too slow to run away from trouble. So I was easy prey for any school-yard bully who needed to express his inner conflicts. To survive, I became a crafty coward, avoiding fights and surviving by my wits. But everywhere I went, a bully always appeared to haunt me. After high school, weighing all of 143 pounds, I enlisted in the army to be a Special Forces medic. I was looking for travel, adventure, and I wanted to learn how to fight. In other words, I was tired of being a coward.

I was put into basic training with a bunch of men from inner-city Newark, New Jersey, who were really tough. Their leader was a fellow named Reid—six feet two, two hundred pounds, and the best street fighter I have ever seen. In just the first few weeks of basic training, I had seen him fight and easily demolish several men, some larger than he, in only seconds.

So, wouldn't you know it? I found myself working with this guy in a crowded, sweaty kitchen as the temperature was reaching 110 degrees. We kept bumping into each other, and tempers flared. Reid stuck his angry face into mine and bellowed for me to get out of his way. I looked him in the eye and decided then and there that I was never going to back down again, even if he killed me. A funny thing happened after that; the look in Reid's eyes softened, and he turned away. And later, as I traveled all around the world, often finding myself in sleazy bars with drunken men trained to fight, no one ever tried to pick a fight with me again, and no one has since.

**My Life as a Tin Man**

If ever there were a scarecrow, it would be my mother. She was softheaded, artistic, emotional, and disorganized—in the words of the Tin Man: that's her all over. And Mom, being an extreme scarecrow, married my Dad, who was as extreme a tin man as you can get. Unemotional, distant, organized, and rational to the point of insanity, Dad failed as a businessman, but became successful as a college professor because of his intellectual brilliance. But he was as difficult to live with as Mom was, and when they divorced for the second time, I stayed with Mom. She became even more chaotic after the separation, and to compensate, I became even more of a tin man. Appropriately, I went into a profession whose motto is "vigilance" because becoming hypervigilant was an important skill in my chaotic world. It made me good at spotting trouble, but it also made it difficult for me to relax.

I can tell you about being a tin man because that has been my main role in life. Being good at it gets you good grades in school, and you can do well in a technical sort of job. I am good at solving problems, and because of this, I enjoy working with groups of young people negotiating challenge courses—helping them learn how to overcome their problems and enjoy the challenge. So, you can be a reasonably successful human being as a tin man, but the role has as many weaknesses as it does strengths.

For one thing, a tin man cannot find a happy ending by himself. If Dorothy had not come along, he would still be stuck in the middle of the forest. Tin men are good at chopping things down and cutting them into pieces. But they cannot put the pieces together to make a new and living creation. So, a tin man can tell the beginning of a story where the characters (pieces) get separated and defined. But he gets stuck in the middle of the story because he cannot bring the pieces together into a new and magical ending. A tin man can only tell an unfinished story (a tragedy), which is why this book was unfinished at the time my mother died. And who wants to read a book about my dead son if you are going to get stuck in the tragedy of it?

Thoughts can be sticky, and tin men, being creatures of thought, are notorious for getting stuck. Our reasoning mind (our tin man) takes our past and splits it up into thoughts, which are naturally attracted to each other—trying to be whole again. It then assembles these thoughts into a safe and stable shelter to view the ever-changing present. Eventually, though, our new experiences accumulate and outgrow this shelter of old ideas—at which point, it falls apart. Then, we either open to what is outside, or our tin man frantically tries to stick our old ideas back together again—getting stuck, himself, in the middle of it all. And that is where I was in the writing of this book—stuck in the middle of the story, in my own unresolved grief. But it was not just the grief for my son that was unfinished. I also needed to heal the loss of my mother and then use her creative power to bring my own story to a conclusion.

When I started my new job at the surgery center, my medical problems went away, and I got my strength back. I now had free time and energy, and I was ready for a new challenge. So, I took my book project down from the shelf and began working on it again. Mom had always encouraged me to write Brian's story, and it was one of the few things we enjoyed talking about. Mom read what I wrote, made suggestions, and was disappointed when I told her that I was giving up on the book.

For most of her life, Mom had been a visual artist—a painter, a decorator, and she dabbled in the theater—but in her later years, she became interested in creative writing. She took several classes, becoming a good writer, and through her stories, I got to know her better. When I read about Mom's childhood, for example, I realized how similar our young lives were—both filled with conflict and separation. By writing about her life, Mom cast a net over its pieces and pulled them together for the reader to see—showing her struggle to be an original human being. And this, I realized, was what I needed to do with my own story. I needed to reveal more parts of myself and let them come together in a new and creative way. I also realized that this was too much of a challenge for me to do alone and that I needed help.

So, now I began writing in a different way. Instead of planning everything, I just asked my story, with all its wonderful characters, to help write itself. If the writing got stuck, I knew I was thinking too much, and so, I would just clear my mind, feel my love for the story, and trust that it would find its way. And as I relaxed and gave up control, the words began flowing onto the paper, growing into sentences that just needed pruning and arranging. The book got better and naturally found its own good ending—people could read it without getting stuck, and I was pleased. Then, as I was finishing the final draft, the red mark on my thigh (like my mother's) went away.

### Happy Endings in Oz

Dorothy begins her journey because of loss. Either she stays at home and loses her dog, or she runs away and loses her family. What can Dorothy do? She cannot see a good solution. Dorothy appears to be stuck. Like Hamlet, her choices are limited because the love in Dorothy's life is limited. But unlike Hamlet, Dorothy wants to go "Over the Rainbow," beyond her limited world. And so, Dorothy gets hit on the head—which quiets her thoughts—allowing her to go beyond the limits of her reasonable mind.

The mystical vortex takes Dorothy to the magical Land of Oz, where she meets powerful forces beyond her understanding. These forces take on the roles of guidance (the Good Witch and the Wizard) and the roles of challenge (the Tin Man, Scarecrow, Lion, and Wicked Witch). Dorothy has "gone to pieces" and is "beside herself" because all of these characters appear to be separate from each other and from Dorothy. But their shared pain tells us that they are all parts of a whole, in need of healing. So, in the course of their many adventures together, the characters draw closer—the Witch providing challenge and giving them someone to unite against.

Finally, the characters band together as one, and this kills the Witch. She is the symbol of their separation and pain—the illusion that appears all-powerful, yet melts away in Dorothy's love for her friends. So, the Witch melts away as the characters' pain and separation melt away. They all find what they were missing, and Dorothy claims the Witch's power. The love that Dorothy was missing in Kansas, she finds in Oz, and it has the power to transform her reality. Dorothy gets the love she had lost and realizes that it was always there for her to find.

## WHEN LOSS BECOMES GRIEF

When we suffer our greatest losses, the ones that take our breath away, we give them a special name. The loss is now so big that instead of it being in us, we are in it—we are in grief. We twist raw in its emptiness, stripped of even our most basic desires. We don't want to eat, don't want to sleep—don't want to even want. It is about all that we can do to even breathe through these moments, and sometimes even this takes a conscious effort.

Most of us can only tolerate this kind of grief every now and then. Our smaller losses, in contrast, can come and go more often. Yet, each kind of loss serves as a marker of sorts. The little ones that pass through us—like stones through water—mark the beginning of a new story in our life. And the big, all-consuming grief that we pass through—like water through a cave—marks the beginning of a new life.

I have always liked the words from the play *Harvey*, when the leading character, Elwood P. Dowd, says, "There are two ways to get through life, being clever or being nice. I've tried being clever and I prefer being nice." Before Brian died, I spent my life being clever, yet found myself alone in a meaningless and tragic world. I did not choose to live in a world more intelligent and creative than I could conceive. I was not a passageway for the unknown—still and empty within. But when Brian died, all this changed. My thoughts became empty, and my heart brimmed over with love. And from this new way of being, a new life grew—one more meaningful and alive than I could have imagined.

## Perfect Grief

When someone dies, some things die, yet something does not die. Anyone who has loved and lost knows this from experience. What die and are grieved are the conditions of the life that is lost: my son/daughter who was young/old, beautiful/plain, sweet/difficult, etc. When someone mourns, it is these conditions that are being mourned, the things we could see and touch. But after death, they go away, one by one, until even the memories of them begin to fade. What is left, if the process is allowed to run its course, is the essence of our beloved. It is the purest form of love, the unconditional and unconditioned. Invisible yet clearly present, it is sometimes gentle, sometimes seething in its creative potential. Having experienced its power and been reminded many times to let go of the conditions of Brian's life, I can be with others who are grieving their own losses. I can feel their love and pain, but I do not suffer with them because I see where their path is leading. They are letting go of their known conditions so they can create something new. Maybe they will lose their fear of death, maybe they will gain new abilities and insights, or their lives will take a new and more creative direction. I do not know what will change. All I know is that healing grief is the most powerful and transforming process I have witnessed.

## Shared Grief

And when the healing process slows to the point where people remain separate, conflicted, and maybe even evil, I know they are holding on to a grief, often unknown to even them. Maybe it is for a lost lover, lost dream, or lost relationship—always grief for a lost condition of love. I also know that if they cannot heal this grief, they will share it. They will hide their pain and pass it off as something else—giving it to someone who, feeling its discomfort, will pass it off again. And so it goes, rippling through our consciousness—coming from everyone suffering a lost love and hiding their pain.

The ripples of grief intermingle and build, growing into waves—the source of Hamlet's "sea of troubles," the Buddha's "samsara," and the restless, unprovoked conflict that troubles our lives. Though hidden, this sea of shared grief has predictable tides and currents, as well as unpredictable rogue waves that arise out of nowhere and pound us with their fury. And though we may not see their source, we can understand that they arise from our shared grief and call us to heal our shared pain.

## "The Singers of Life"

One day, anthropologist Loren Eiseley leaned against a stump at the edge of a small glade and fell asleep.

When I awoke, dimly aware of some commotion and outcry in the clearing, the light was slanting down through the pines in such a way that the glade was lit like some vast cathedral. I could see the dust motes of wood pollen in the long shaft of light, and there on the extended branch sat an enormous raven with a red and squirming nestling in his beak.

The sound that awoke me was the outraged cries of the nestling's parents, who flew helplessly in circles about the clearing. The sleek back monster was indifferent to them. He gulped, wetted his beak on the dead branch a moment, and sat still. Up to that point, the little tragedy had followed the usual pattern. But suddenly, out of all that area of woodland, a soft sound of complaint began to rise. Into the glade fluttered small birds of half a dozen varieties drawn by the anguished outcries of the tiny parents.

No one dared to attack the raven. But they cried there in some instinctive common misery. The bereaved and the unbereaved. The glade filled with their soft rustling and their cries. They fluttered as though to point their wings at the murderer. There was a dim and tangible ethic he had violated, that they knew. He was a bird of death.

And he, the murderer, the black bird at the heart of life, sat on there, glistening in the formidable, unmoving, unperturbed, untouchable.

The sighing died. It was then I saw the judgment. It was the judgment of life over death. I will never see it again so forcefully presented. I will never hear it again in notes so tragically prolonged. For in the midst of protest, they forgot the violence. There, in that clearing, the crystal note of a song sparrow lifted hesitantly in the hush. And finally, after painful fluttering, another took the song, and then another, the song passing from one bird to another, doubtfully at first, as though some evil thing was being slowly forgotten. Until suddenly they took heart and sang from many throats joyously together as birds are known to sing. They sang because life is sweet and sunlight beautiful. They sang under the brooding shadow of the raven. In the simple truth they had forgotten the raven, for they were the singers of life, and not of death.[1]

> Whence shall he have grief,
> how shall he be deluded
> who sees everywhere the Oneness?
> —*Isha Upanishad*

---

1   From THE IMMENSE JOURNEY by Loren Eiseley, copyright 1946, 1950, 1951, 1953, 1955, 1956, 1957 by Loren Eiseley. Used by permission of Random House, Inc.

Our emptiness calls us to heal
and gives us a birthing place,
for what we cannot imagine
and what we could not face.

# Chapter 6
# Magical Child

I HAVE BEEN FORTUNATE to find help in unfolding the mystery surrounding Brian's life and death. Much of this has come through Bob Monroe and the folks at The Monroe Institute—one of the few places where I can find people with interests and experiences similar to mine. But there is one person who has been particularly helpful to me, and before this, he was a mentor to Bob Monroe. This fellow settled here long ago and introduced Bob to this area, and he became my teacher and friend.

## SOMEONE WHO UNDERSTANDS

One day, my friend Scott, the bicycle mechanic, introduced me to his father-in-law and next-door neighbor, a grey, wrinkled little man with bright, smiling eyes named Joseph Chilton Pearce. Joe, it turned out, was quite a find: budding composer turned college professor turned author and lecturer. Joe was a friend of Carlos Castaneda, Bob Monroe, and just about every noted mystic in the West, and he was a student of Muktananda—one of the famous teachers from the East. Joe has also authored many influential books, including his classics, *The Crack in the Cosmic Egg* and *Magical Child*.

Now if there was anyone on this planet who could help me understand a magical child like Brian, it was Joe Pearce—and explain he did. I would visit him in his hand-built home and listen as he told me stories of his adventures all around the world. By this time, I had read many biographies of famous people, mystical and not, but none of their stories could hold a candle to Joe's. "Joe," I told him, "you should write an autobiography so other people can learn from your experiences, like I am doing."

But he just waved his hand in the air and said, "Naah."

Joe's mind was as brilliant as his stories, and the knowledge flowed out of him in torrents, faster than I could absorb. He spoke of anthropological studies from primitive cultures, state-of-the-art developmental biology, and his own mystical experiences—all weaving a picture of a world much different than I had understood. It is a reality much more fluid, intelligent, and interesting than most people realize. And at its heart is Joe's favorite subject, the physical and spiritual development of children.

"We need to listen to the children," Joe says. "They are our teachers." They provide a natural link to a vast nonphysical intelligence. We teach them how to live in the physical world, and they teach us how to learn and grow beyond our current understanding. Children naturally carry the wisdom we need to solve our problems, but most people do not recognize this. If we did, we would cultivate this resource—nurturing their wonderful ability to imagine new ideas. We could cultivate their creative ability, but instead, we are burying it. The problems with our child-raising, Joe relates, are severalfold.

First, breastfeeding for at least a year, preferably two, along with continual mother-baby contact during the first six months is of great importance for healthy child development. Joe says we are raising some of the loneliest, most disconnected children in history because we do not meet their basic human needs. One of the consequences is that the process of imagination is squashed when children are disconnected from their natural source of love and safety. In order to imagine, you must feel safe, and most children are separated from their mothers during their early years—their best source of love, safety, and nourishment.

As children grow older, they need natural, playful, and uncontrolled interactions that lead to new ideas. But instead, we give them the isolating, controlled violence of television for, on average, four hours a day. This creates problems because when you give children TV pictures instead of written or spoken words, they do not create pictures in their heads—they do not imagine. And when they do not imagine, they cannot express their natural creativity. The unfortunate result is that when this creative force is blocked and contained, it often becomes destructive and violent.

The next especially vulnerable time for development is adolescence when children are, in effect, getting new bodies again. This is when they need continued safety, connection, support, and role models from family and community. But it is a time when most adolescents are deprived of these. Also, because teenagers are healthy and strong, brimming over with energy and ideas, they are often frustrated by an inability to express their creative talents through meaningful work.

Another problem, Joe relates, is that our culture does not recognize the concept of nonphysical intelligence. We teach our children that there are no miracles and no magic. Our institutions filter out any mention of this from the media (as was the case with Brian's story), from education, and even from most religions. Children learn at an early age that this natural, creative part of themselves cannot be expressed if they are to be accepted. Instead, we teach them to bury it, and when they do, we do not even recognize their grief.

Joe speaks of these problems with passion. His beloved children are being injured by society, and Joe is concerned. Like many gifted people who can see through the ignorance of their time, Joe has been faced with two choices: withdraw from society or confront its ignorance. And Joe has managed to do both—living simply with his family and growing much of his own food, while every few weeks, launching himself around the world to lecture at cutting-edge conferences on child development. From Rangoon to Rio, Joe has said what he knows to be true to those willing to listen. It is not easy being ahead of your time, but I believe Joe has done a good job of it.

One thing that Joe has learned from all his travels is that there are other children like Brian, all around the world, and they seem to be popping up more frequently than before. Educators say that these gifted new children act "like they are from another planet," and their schools do not know what to do with them. Some of these children even call themselves "the new children" and say they have come to help us. Whatever your view on these ideas, I would like to share a few more examples of how children I have known have shown a natural intelligence.

When our second son, Matthew, was four years old, I was taking an IQ test I found in a magazine. There was one question (by far the hardest, requiring a one-in-a-million IQ above 150) that I could not figure out, even after seeing the correct answer. It was a complicated geometrical progression of colors and proportions. So, as Matthew walked by, I asked him to look at the problem and its six possible answers. He glanced over at it and said matter-of-factly, "B" (the correct answer).

"How did you know that?" I asked.

"I don't know," he replied.

A few weeks later, I was filling out a school application for Matthew and asked him to weigh himself on the bathroom scale. He disappeared for a few minutes and then came back with the information, "a three and a zero," he said. (He could not count to thirty.) A few hours later, I was filling out an insurance application as Matthew came by and watched me write down my weight as 180 pounds. "Oh, six Matthews," he said. Yet, two years later, he still did not know how to perform multiplication or division.

My daughter, Lyn, who has many mental disabilities and even at the age of fifteen could not tie her shoelaces will, about once a year, come over to me when I am struggling to fix something and show me how to do it. "Here, Daddy, use this," she will say, handing me the correct tool. If we find an old key, Lyn can identify it in an instant. (She says she remembers the notches.) And when we got a new puppy, she always seemed to know when it was going to pee on the floor. "He gonna go pee-pee!" she would proclaim at the top of her lungs a few minutes before he did.

Lyn had a friend over one day who was flirting with Matthew. As a result of all the extra attention, Matthew started acting goofy and managed to spill five pounds of sugar down the stairs. (Don't ask me why.) This came at the end of a busy weekend. Kathryn was out of town, and as a single parent, I was exhausted. "Just what I don't need," I said in annoyance, "another cleanup job to do!" I got out the vacuum cleaner, but Matthew was standing in my way, wide-eyed and confused. "The least you can do is get out of my way," I said. But he only moved a few feet and was soon in my way again. "Get out of my way!" I yelled, and he ran into the next room and slammed the door.

Angrily, I worked my way down the stairs until a few moments later, Matthew appeared above me, eyes moist with tears. "But you don't understand," he said so genuinely that I stopped vacuuming and looked up at him. "Someday, I'll grow up and move away, and if we don't take care of this now, we may never do it."

"Yes," I said, feeling myself soften, "I think you're right. What should we do?"

"We should apologize," Matthew said. So we each took turns apologizing, Matthew for making the mess and me for getting angry at him. He had been in my way because he was trying to figure out how to help me but just did not know what to do, he said.

"What should we do next?" I asked him.

"You should teach me to use the vacuum cleaner so I can clean up the sugar," and so I did. We worked well together, and in a few minutes, the job was done. Then I told Matthew how much I appreciated his courage in coming into my anger and the wisdom of his suggestions. I listened to Matthew, and as a result, we solved the problem and grew closer together.

When Matthew was in kindergarten, I used to visit his class to tell stories and play games with the children. Sometimes I would play intuition games, just to let the kids know that—with me at least—it was okay to express this part of themselves. To prepare a game, I took a childhood picture of a mass murderer, circled it, and put it in an envelope marked with an "A" on the outside. Then I took pictures of Matthew and Brian (I always try to create links to Brian; it helps me get better results), circled Matthew's picture, and put it into an envelope with "B" on the outside.

I then told the children the story of how the founder of Sony Electronics used his intuition to make better business decisions. After he used his brain to make the best possible deal, he would use his belly to make his final decision. He would imagine "eating" the deal and see how it felt in his belly. If it felt good, he would take the deal, and if it felt bad, he would refuse it. Next, I told the children to imagine that they had two offers to have a play date with two kids that they did not know well, both for the same time. They were going to use their bellies to decide which one to play with. I told them that the two kids' pictures were circled inside the two sealed envelopes, which I then showed them.

"Now close your eyes, and imagine you are eating envelope A." After a few seconds, I told them to keep their eyes closed and raise their hand if it felt good. Two hands went up out of thirteen children. Then

I asked for the hands of those whose bellies felt bad. Nine hands went up. I repeated the same process with envelope B (Matthew's picture) and got twelve "goods" and one "bad." When I opened the envelopes and explained whom the pictures were of, the teacher put her hands to her face and said, "Oh, my goodness!" But the children just asked for another story; it was no surprise to them.

My final example of child wisdom occurred when Kathryn and I returned home one evening after having dinner out. Our babysitter, a wonderful girl of twelve whose father is a fundamentalist Christian minister, had told the children Bible stories and about how you go to hell when you are bad. "Things come out and grab you!" she said proudly, pinching her fingers together. I did not like this, so I told her in front of the children that some stories are okay with me, but I do not want the children to hear stories, watch TV shows, or be around people who are trying to make them afraid. It was a little awkward, but I did not speak in anger, which helped get the idea across.

A few minutes later, after Kathryn left to take the sitter home, Matthew asked, "Is hell real?"

"Yes," I answered, "it is a real thought, a real possibility, maybe even a real dream. Not a place I care to spend my time, though."

Then Matthew pointed to his hand and said, "I see a hook trying to stick into my hand."

"I call that a daydream," I said.

"How do I make it go away?" Matthew asked.

"If you push it away, it will just push back. It is trying to teach you something. Make it feel welcome, and ask what it wants."

After a few seconds, Matthew spoke, "It says don't get hooked by a dream—and now it's gone."

"Kid," I said, "you're good."

Both Brian and Joe Pearce taught me to listen to the children, and my life has been better for it. Though Joe is one of the brightest and most knowledgeable people I know, it is his open-mindedness and willingness to learn that most impressed me. Because of this, as I began to have more of my own ideas and experiences, our visits became more of a dialogue. Joe would talk for an hour, and then I would chime in for a few minutes. But it was always fun, and I appreciated his company and felt appreciated by him. It is a wonderful thing to have a friend like Joe, who understands. It makes me wonder, though, how it was for Brian when he was alive. How hard it must have been for him, a child of nine, surrounded by adults who did not understand that he had a foot in both worlds, or even that there is another world. Sometimes I wish I could go back in time and be a better father and friend to Brian, especially in his darkest times. I wish I could have known then what I know now. But rather than living for the past, longing for a day that will never come, I am doing my best to stay in the present. That is where, I think, Brian would want me. And I know it may sound strange, but I feel that he is still around. Sometimes I feel him when I look into a child's eyes or see the sparkling leaves of a fall tree. I feel the love we shared in the vortex, and I know he is here, in one way or another, and that everything is all right.

One Christmas when Matthew was five, he crawled into my lap and asked me a question, "Daddy, is there really a Santa Claus?" I remembered how, at about the same age, Brian had asked me the same question and how I hemmed and hawed, trying but failing to find the right words. I sidestepped the question, and Brian turned away from me, disappointed. So when I looked into Matthew's eyes, I saw Brian's too, and I finally understood what they were really asking:

"Daddy, do you believe in magic? Is it okay if I do?"

"Will you still love me, even if I do things you can't understand?"

"Daddy, can I be a magical child?"

I looked into Matthew's eyes and realized that I was getting a second chance to answer this deep and heartfelt question. *Maybe I can do a better job this time,* I thought. So, now, I did not try to find the words. Instead, I surrendered to the love I felt for both my sons, and the words came to me.

"Yes, Santa and his friends are real, just not physical. Only *we* are physical, though. Only *we* give them life."

Matthew smiled up at me, obviously relieved. "I thought so," he said and scampered off to play in another room.

## FALL HARVEST

It is fall now. Many years have passed since I wrote the first chapter of this book, and the leaves are in their full splendor again. Our four old apple trees have been very thoughtful. The first year after Brian died they bore large, delicious apples for the first time in our twelve years here. Then, the next year, they produced nothing. At that time, though, we knew that Kathryn was pregnant with our new son, Matthew. He was born the following January, one week after Brian's birthday, and everything had gone perfectly. Lyn delighted in having a little brother she could take care of, and when Matthew was a toddler, they slept together in each other's arms. Lyn says she has two brothers now: Matthew, who is here with us now, and Brian, who is in heaven. For most people, Brian has been forgotten, but he is still alive in our hearts.

When Matthew was eighteen months old, he saw a photograph on the floor taken of Brian shortly before his death. Matthew pointed to the photo excitedly—saying, "Kiyee! Kiyee!" That seemed to be his name for Brian. When we asked questions about Brian, Matthew nodded his head yes or no (he only spoke a little) and seemed to know more about Brian than we would have expected.

"Where is Kiyee?" Kathryn asked.

"Kiyee in cassroom," Matthew answered.

"You mean classroom?" Kathryn asked, and Matthew nodded his head, yes. (A classroom is commonly described in near-death experiences, and Brian had recently appeared to Kathryn in a dream, walking down our road while reading a book.)

Matthew is very bright (like everyone else's child, I realize), and because of our experience with Brian, we are better able to recognize his needs and help him learn and grow. It seems as though Brian prepared a way for him into our lives. I can say, and others have told me, that I am a better father than I was to Brian—more patient and loving. I wish I could have done better for Brian, but it was the best I could do at the time. Now, maybe I can pass on some of what Brian has taught me to Matthew. I also wonder what new things Matthew has in store to teach me.

The apple trees helped celebrate our joy at Matthew's birth by giving us another bumper crop of large, delicious apples. The weight of the lush fruit was too much for one of the old ones to bear, and it fell over—bringing delight to the deer who could now reach all the ripe apples, not just the ones on the lower branches. I watched the deer feast from its dying limbs as it offered its final gifts to this world. It reminded me of Brian. After it was gone, we planted a strong new tree in its place. And now there are four again—as we are four again with Matthew. The trees have been very kind to us.

I had always thought that death was the worst thing that could happen and to overcome its fear was the ultimate in earthly courage. But this no longer seems to be true. Both death and life are just different ways of being. Like all the other phases of our existence, they complement each other. We struggle during our waking hours, and in sleep, we are rested and renewed while our dreams give us guidance and reflection. Spring and summer are times of great activity while fall and winter are periods of preparation, rest, and drawing together. And so, when Brian ran home on that beautiful spring day, it was in joy that he bridged his own two worlds. And those of us who loved him felt our lives changing, too. We were now a little less separate, a little less afraid, and better at facing our own challenges.

There are many things that I thought Brian took with him when he died. I thought I lost his friendship, but it has been returned to me manyfold in the friendships that now arise without effort. And the easier they come, the less I seem to need them. I miss his laughter, but in truth, Brian struggled as much as he laughed; though when he did laugh, he was brilliant. And now we have Matthew, for whom life comes so easily. He struggles very little and laughs a lot, and when he does, he will cock his head and roll his eyes dramatically, and it will be Brian's exact expression we see, grinning at us. In truth, there is some Brian in Matthew, and we encourage him to laugh as much as he can, because to us, it sounds like the laughter of angels.

But of all the losses, what I miss the most are Brian's words. They reveal a beauty and mystery that he saw more clearly than I. Brian was such a clear being that the beauty of his words flowed through rather than from him. And now I see that something has changed for me here, too. I am beginning to write poetry, which I could never do before. And sometimes now, my heart will open, and I will write something that feels beautiful, and I will wonder where it is coming from. Then I will feel a peace and wholeness that makes me think that there is some Brian in the beauty of the words that are now flowing through me.

Recently, I have noticed that the flow of time has begun to dull my memory of Brian. I need to look at pictures and videos to remind me of how he looked and sounded—how he made us laugh and filled our lives with poetry and imagination. But there is nothing to remind me of how he felt and smelled. *When even his memories are gone, I wondered, what will be left? The empty place in my heart that was Brian—so precious, how could I let it go?*

So, I continued to grieve, and one day, finding myself alone, I allowed myself to grieve deeply. My sadness rose up in building waves until the tears flowed out in racking sobs, feeling good—so clean and open—releasing itself into words: "Brian, I miss you so much. What will I do without you? Who will teach me? Who will love me as I am, now that you're gone?"

And then the warmth and love in my heart grew so strong that it seemed to burst open. Everything went black, and these words took form in a crashing wave of emotion:

*I will always love you.*

*Through me you will learn to love all things, all things as me.*

*I am no longer the dead body on the table.*

*All the things you wanted, thought you needed from me, from outside yourself, lay dead on the table. They were the creation of your own thoughts and needs, created by you and for you with the greatest love and care.*

*I was a stepping-stone in the river, to be stepped on lightly and in passing.*

*I was the body, was the stone ... I am the river.*

*I will always love you.*

And with these words came an all-encompassing love, and an understanding. This was the rippling river of energy waves I had seen and felt with Lyn the night Brian died. And it is this river, coursing through my emptiness, that contains what I had known as Brian, and of which I now longed to be a conscious part.

Sometimes, when children leave home, their parents forget to practice the lessons their children have taught them. They usually do not realize that what they have been teaching their children—how to act and think like an adult—is often not as important as what their children have been teaching them—how to learn and grow as a child. It is so easy to hold on to our grief and stay like we are. Sometimes, we are reminded that there is more for us, and that keeps us on our journey. Sometimes, we are reminded by a child.

*Gregg Korbon*

Brian (age three) and
Dad at the beach

Dancing on the sand

Brian (four months old) with Kathryn

Matthew (age two)

Brian with little sister, Lyn

# Epilogue

A FULL FIFTEEN YEARS went into the making of this book. During that time, our son, Matt, was born and is now thirteen. He goes to a school for gifted children (The Peabody School—named after the dog genius, Mr. Peabody, from the *Rocky and Bullwinkle* cartoon show), and this has been a good place for Matt. I always assumed that he would be a math and science guy like me, but while Matt is good at these, it is his writing that is his strongest talent. Sometimes, it is so good that his teachers wonder if his work is plagiarized, but it isn't. Matt just writes from a place so deep and rich that few people go, and Kathryn and I try to keep him safe along the way. One more year at Peabody and then Matt will go on to public high school, which will offer many new challenges. So, we are keeping our fingers crossed for him.

Our special needs daughter, Lyn, is twenty-one and getting ready to leave the shelter of the public school system to, hopefully, find a good job. Lyn has been an adventure for us all, and Kathryn has been the most inspiring of moms. The experts told us that Lyn would never read, but Kathryn taught her to read. They told us that Lyn would never write, but Kathryn taught her how to do that, too. Add to that twelve years of potty training (equivalent to 120 normal children, we figured) and countless daily challenges, and it is a wonder that Lyn seems to be turning out all right. She is one of the happiest people I know and has a chance to get a good job working with her friends at the university. The big turning point in the lives of mentally handicapped people is whether or not they can find meaningful work. So, we are keeping our fingers crossed for her, too.

Kathryn, despite enduring so much stress and trauma throughout the years, has aged well. She is a true worker bee and continues to amaze me with her stamina and grit. Besides Kathryn's pastoral counseling practice and church and parenting responsibilities, she also works for the State of Virginia, helping overwhelmed mothers get services for their special needs children. I tease her that she has the perfect job: getting paid to talk on the phone while helping grateful moms. But while Kathryn has generally done well, she has had two ongoing problems. The first was the idea that I would never finish writing this book—sporadically disappearing into my office for hours at a time, year after year, with no end in sight. "Sorry, honey, I'd like to, but I have to work on my book."

Kathryn's second chronic concern was that I *would* finish this book and then get it published. This idea bothered her because she always considered Brian's story to be a private matter and never liked the idea of the media distorting the truth like they had in the past. Either the television, newspaper, or radio stories told only a few mundane facts, leaving out the wonder, or they changed the story to suit their own needs: "Knowing he was dying of terminal heart disease, Brian stumbled bravely around the bases, gasping for air and then collapsing across home plate," (told on national radio). These distortions were hurtful, and we felt betrayed by their dishonesty. So our true story remained in limbo for many years.

As a result, my writing tablet was my first, and for a long time, my only audience. Its pages accepted my pencil marks on its surface and my tears into its layers. So much happened with Brian, more than I can describe here, and yet I understood so little. So I kept writing to better remember and understand. But I was also aware that Brian's story wanted to be told.

A year into the writing, as I finished the first chapter, I told Kathryn that I thought it would be a good story for *Reader's Digest*. A few hours later, I got a call from a writer who had read about the ball field dedication and wanted to write an article about Brian for *Reader's Digest*. But I read some of his work and did not think he would write the story the way it should be done. So nothing happened.

A year after that, as I finished the second chapter, I mentioned to Kathryn that I thought Brian's story would make a good movie. The next day, I got a call from a writer who had heard a little about the story and wanted to make it into a movie. He wrote a proposal and tried to sell it, but after a few months, he said it did not work out. So nothing happened, again.

Then twelve years later, after I finally finished the last chapter of this book, the story began to find its live audience. One day, Kathryn, Matt, and I were walking on the downtown mall after Matt's last day of fifth grade, looking for a place to eat lunch. We saw a silver trailer with a sign by the door that said, "StoryCorps," parked in front of a coffeehouse. I poked my head inside and asked the young man and woman, sitting at a small table, what they were doing. "We record people's stories," they said. So I told them that I had a story to tell; whereupon, they informed me that you had to make an appointment a week in advance, but it just so happened that they had a cancellation and could take us right now. So, Kathryn and Matt joined me in the trailer as I told Brian's story publicly for the first time. This was also the first time that Matt had heard it, and tears ran down his face as he listened.

A few months later, I got an e-mail from the local National Public Radio station saying that our story would be part of a special one-hour broadcast that night. So we listened to the WMRA StoryCorps Special and were pleased that they gave our story the last twenty minutes of the show. Some people in our community told us they heard the radio program when they were in their cars and were touched by the story, so much that they had to pull over and stop. Later that year, our story was included in the StoryCorps book, *Listening Is an Act of Love*, by Dave Isay, the founder of StoryCorps. He sent us a copy of the book inscribed with a thoughtful note thanking us for participating in his project. Then, as a result of our positive experience with StoryCorps and in an act of trust, Kathryn gave this book her blessing.

So here it is, our experience with a gifted child who spent time with us, died, and yet remains a presence in our lives. Would I ever choose to have Brian born as he was, suffer as he did, and then die in my arms? No, never—that would not be reasonable. Brian's life was clearly beyond anything I would call "reasonable." I think that Kathryn did not want me to tell our story because she knew that if I explained it—made it reasonable—I could destroy its power to transform. But I cannot explain Brian. I can just tell you about the still unfolding mystery of his life and his death. So I am grateful that Brian spent time with us and gave us so much to wonder about. I am pleased to be Brian's father, to love and learn from him, and now to share our story.

and so, our story is done
a life well lived, my son

# Resources

www.BeyondReason.info

Visit our Web site to learn more about our story, order copies of *Beyond Reason*, share stories of loss and healing, and share unusual occurrences associated with the loss of a loved one.

The Compassionate Friends

A helpful organization providing support to families grieving the death of a child.

The Compassionate Friends, Inc.
P.O. Box 3696
Oak Brook, IL 60522-3696
Toll-free: 877-969-0010
Phone: 630-990-0010
Fax: 630-990-0246
www.compassionatefriends.org

The Monroe Institute

A center for the exploration and transformation of human consciousness, located south of Charlottesville, Virginia.

*Gregg Korbon*

The Monroe Institute
365 Roberts Mountain Road
Faber, VA 22938
Toll-free: 866-881-3440
Phone: 434-361-1252
Fax: 434-361-1237
www.monroeinstitute.com

# Bibliography

Almas, A. H. *The Void: Inner Spaciousness and Ego Structure.* Berkeley, CA: Diamond Books, 1992.

Atwater, F. Holmes. *Captain of My Ship, Master of My Soul: Living with Guidance.* Charlottesville, VA: Hampton Roads, 2001.

Barks, Coleman, and John Moyne, trans. *The Essential Rumi.* New York: HarperCollins, 1995.

Bauval, Robert. *The Egypt Code.* New York: The Disinformation Co., 2008.

Bowlby, John. *Loss: Sadness and Depression.* New York: Basic Books, 1980.

Campbell, Joseph. *Myths to Live By: How We Re-Create Ancient Legends in our Daily Lives to Release Human Potential.* New York: Bantam Books, 1972.

Carse, James P. *Finite and Infinite Games.* New York: Ballantine Books, 1986.

Castaneda, Carlos. *The Power of Silence: Further Lessons of don Juan.* New York: Simon & Schuster, 1987.

Cori, Jasmin Lee. *Healing from Trauma: A Survivor's Guide to Understanding Your Symptoms and Reclaiming Your Life.* New York: Marlowe & Co., 2007.

Davis, John. *The Diamond Approach: An Introduction to the Teachings of A. H. Almas.* Boston: Shambala, 1999.

Dossey, Larry, MD. *Healing Words: The Power of Prayer and the Practice of Medicine.* New York: HarperCollins, 1993.

Eiseley, Loren C. *The Immense Journey.* New York: Random House, 1957.

Gordon, Stuart. *The Encyclopedia of Myths and Legends.* London: Headline Book Publishing, 1993.

Hall, Manley P. *The Secret Teachings of All Ages.* Charleston, SC: Forgotten Books, 2008.

Hancock, Graham. *Fingerprints of the Gods.* New York: Three Rivers Press, 1996.

———. *Supernatural: Meetings with the Ancient Teachers.* New York: The Disinformation Co., 2007.

Haramein, Nassim. *Crossing the Event Horizon: Rise to the Equation.* Symposium DVD Set, 2007, www.theresonanceproject.org.

Hart, Tobin. *The Secret Spiritual World of Children.* Novato, CA: New World Library, 2003.

Hawking, Stephen, and Roger Penrose. *The Nature of Space and Time.* Princeton: Princeton University Press, 1996.

Isaacson, Walter. *Einstein: His Life and Universe.* New York: Simon & Schuster, 2008.

Isay, Dave. *Listening Is an Act of Love: A Celebration of American Life from the StoryCorps Project.* New York: Penguin Press, 2007.

Johnson, Robert A. *Inner Work: Using Dreams and Active Imagination for Personal Growth.* New York: HarperOne, 1989.

Jung, Carl G., ed. *Man and His Symbols.* New York: Dell, 1964.

Kübler-Ross, Elizabeth. *On Death and Dying.* New York: Simon & Schuster, 1970.

———. *On Children and Death.* New York: Macmillan, 1993.

Levine, Stephen. *Healing into Life and Death.* New York: Doubleday, 1987.

McCraty, Rollin. "The Energetic Heart: Bioelectromagnetic Communication Within and Between People." In *Clinical*

*Applications of Bioelectronic Medicine.* New York: Marcel Dekker, 2004.

McMoneagle, Joseph. *Remote Viewing Secrets: A Handbook.* Charlottesville, VA: Hampton Roads, 2000.

———. *Memoirs of a Psychic Spy: The Remarkable Life of U.S. Government Remote Viewer 001.* Charlottesville, VA: Hampton Roads, 2008.

Monroe, Robert A. *Far Journeys.* New York: Doubleday, 1985.

———. *Journeys Out of the Body.* New York: Doubleday, 1971.

———. *Ultimate Journey.* New York: Doubleday, 1994.

Pearce, Joseph Chilton. *The Crack in the Cosmic Egg.* Rochester, VT: Park Street Press, 2002.

———. *The Death of Religion and the Rebirth of Spirit: A Return to the Intelligence of the Heart.* Rochester, VT: Park Street Press, 2007.

———. *Evolution's End: Claiming the Potential of Our Intelligence.* New York: HarperCollins, 1992.

———. *Magical Child.* New York: Plume, 1992.

Prigogine, Ilya. *The End of Certainty: Time, Chaos, and the New Laws of Nature.* New York: The Free Press, 1996.

Radin, Dean. *The Conscious Universe: The Scientific Truth of Psychic Phenomena.* New York: HarperOne, 1997.

———. *Entangled Minds: Extrasensory Experience in a Quantum Reality.* New York: Paraview Pocket Books, 2006.

Rinpoche, Sogyal. *The Tibetan Book of Living and Dying.* New York: HarperCollins, 1992.

Rosenblum, Bruce. *Quantum Enigma: Physics Encounters Consciousness.* New York: Oxford University Press USA, 2008.

Russell, Peter. *From Science to God.* Novato, CA: New World Library, 2003.

———. *The Global Brain: The Awakening Earth in a New Century.* Edinburgh, Scotland: Floris Books, 2008.

Scaer, Robert. *The Trauma Spectrum: Hidden Wounds and Human Resiliency.* New York: W. W. Norton & Co., 2005.

Schneider, Michael S. *A Beginner's Guide to Constructing the Universe: The Mathematical Archetypes of Nature, Art, and Science.* New York: HarperCollins, 1994.

Sheldrake, Rupert. *Dogs That Know When Their Masters Are Coming Home and Other Unexplained Powers of Animals.* New York: Three Rivers Press, 2000.

———. *The Sense of Being Stared At and Other Unexplained Powers of the Human Mind.* New York: Three Rivers Press, 2004.

Shlain, Leonard. *Art & Physics: Parallel Visions in Space, Time, and Light.* New York: HarperCollins, 2007.

Sitchin, Zecharia. *Journeys to the Mythical Past.* Rochester, VT: Bear & Co., 2007.

Smith, Huston. *The World's Religions: Our Great Wisdom Traditions.* New York: HarperCollins, 1991.

Talbot, Michael. *The Holographic Universe.* New York: Harper Perennial, 1992.

Tammet, Daniel. *Born on a Blue Day: Inside the Extraordinary Mind of an Autistic Savant.* New York: The Free Press, 2006.

Taylor, Richard P. "Order in Pollock's Chaos." *Scientific American.* Dec (2002): 116–121.

Thompson, Chic. *What a Great Idea! 2.0: Unlocking Your Creativity in Business and in Life.* New York: Sterling Publishing Co., 2007.

Thurston, Mark. *The Essential Edgar Cayce.* New York: Tarcher, 2004.

Tompkins, Peter. *Mysteries of the Mexican Pyramids.* New York: Thames & Hudson Ltd., 1987.

Travis, John W., and Regina Sara Ryan. *Wellness Workbook: How to Achieve Enduring Health and Vitality.* Berkeley, CA: Celestial Arts, 2004.

Treffert, Darold A. *Extraordinary People: Understanding Savant Syndrome.* 2006. www.backinprint.com.

Underhill, Evelyn. *Mysticism.* 12th ed. New York: Doubleday, 1990.

Watterson, Bill. *The Complete Calvin and Hobbes.* Kansas City, MO: Andrew McMeel Publishing, 2005.

Weil, Andrew. *Spontaneous Healing.* New York: Ballantine Books, 2000.

Wolf, Fred Alan. *Dr. Quantum's Little Book of Big Ideas: Where Science Meets Spirit.* Needham, MA: Moment Point Press, 2005.

Wolinsky, Stephen. *Trances People Live: Healing Approaches in Quantum Psychology.* Las Vegas, NV: Bramble Books, 1991.

# About the Author

GREGG KORBON ENLISTED IN the army after high school and served as an artillery officer during the Vietnam era. He then attended Duke University and Duke University School of Medicine, specializing in anesthesiology and pain management. Dr. Korbon taught at Duke and the University of Virginia medical schools, entered private practice, and now directs an outpatient surgery center. He has authored books and research articles and developed new techniques that are widely used in his field.

Dr. Korbon has also had a long-standing interest in outdoor education and is a senior facilitator at the University of Virginia's Poplar Ridge challenge course. While an undergraduate at Duke, he created a weeklong adventure course for incoming freshmen, now called Project W.I.L.D. (Wilderness Initiative Learning at Duke), which became a model for many university outdoor programs. He holds a black belt in tae kwon do, a brown belt in judo, and has logged over forty thousand miles as a bicycle commuter. Dr. Korbon has known challenge and pain, but it was only through the death of his son that he found their common source. He lives in the Blue Ridge Mountains of central Virginia with his wife and children.